Scenarios in Public Administration

Critical Thinking Exercises

Robert J. Daniello
Paulette Laubsch

UNIVERSITY PRESS OF AMERICA, ® INC.
Lanham • Boulder • New York • Toronto • Plymouth, UK

Copyright © 2008 by
University Press of America,® Inc.
4501 Forbes Boulevard
Suite 200
Lanham, Maryland 20706
UPA Acquisitions Department (301) 459-3366

Estover Road
Plymouth PL6 7PY
United Kingdom

Library of Congress Control Number: 2008926477
ISBN-13: 978-0-7618-4086-2 (paperback : alk. paper)
ISBN-10: 0-7618-4086-9 (paperback : alk. paper)
eISBN-13: 978-0-7618-4176-0
eISBN-10: 0-7618-4176-8

™ The paper used in this publication meets the minimum
requirements of American National Standard for Information
Sciences—Permanence of Paper for Printed Library Materials,
ANSI Z39.48—1984

Contents

Foreword

This book, despite its comparatively small size, makes a significant contribution to learning.

Beginning with the title, one is intrigued by the authors' use of the word "scenario." Upon reflection, one can see how the use of this word differs so much from the more prevalent "case" or "case studies." Cases and case studies tend to be linear. Typically, they relate to some specific body of knowledge, competency, concept, organizational auspice, theory, and so forth. So a "case" is written around some specific topic or sub-topic. For example, if a desired learning outcome relates to, say, participatory decision making, the "case" will focus on this. While this methodology certainly can spawn discussion and learning, it does not portray reality sufficiently and, consequently, has limited efficacy as a teaching and learning strategy. Drs. Daniello and Laubsch have transcended such compartmentalized thinking in this volume.

Each of the scenarios has a genre or key point, however, individual and group discussions about respective scenarios can be far reaching; more based on workplace realities; more open to learners from a broad array of backgrounds and; more interesting. Not putting these scenarios under respective headings, subsections, or topic classifications was ingenious.

The phrase "situational management" has by now taken on characteristics of cliché. Although numerous authors have articulated paradigms for understanding "situations," the fact of the matter is that each situation is unique, but not such that there is no way to ground our thoughts and actions. This is probably the major challenge of teaching and learning in government and not-for-profit sector administration and management. At one extreme a learner could throw up her or his hands and say this management stuff is just luck or art, lurking within an anarchistic, kaleidoscopic world; and perhaps some of it is.

Or, one could go to the opposite extreme and portray each dimension of administrative/management science as fitting neatly into X number of class sessions; then one takes another course in some myopic sub-topic for Y class sessions; and on until some degree or certificate is awarded. A thesis, project, or capstone of some kind can help students integrate, however this, typically, comes at the end and the student may not be sufficiently prepared to take on this complicated task of integration and systems thinking. It is here that Robert Daniello and Paulette Laubsch make a major contribution. The situations presented herein really are "situational." Instructors who use this book will enjoy the rich discussions that these stories will surely generate and students will have a rare opportunity to see things in a systematic, albeit complex and reality-based, way as they are progressing through their studies.

It is obvious that the authors have "been around the block." The array of issues potentially addressable in these scenarios includes virtually every dimension of administrative/management science. They allow the reader to see the complex relationships involved with the system of government in The United States that is an exemplar of federalism. The scenarios can be analyzed along the spectrum from micro to macro perspectives. Finally, the scenarios can be used to illustrate the economic, interpersonal, legal, political, social, and technological challenges and opportunities faced by the public sector manager. And they do all this with such clarity and brevity!

Dr. Robert Daniello and Dr. Paulette Laubsch have made a major contribution to education and training in administrative/management science in government.

Richard Blake, Ph.D.
Professor
Seton Hall University

Preface

Jane Jacobs in her seminal work entitled, *The Death and Life of Great American Cities* (1961), declared that cities are virtual laboratories of trial and error, failure, and success. They are the focal points for experimentation, investigation, and observation where formulation, implementation, and evaluation should take place. Perhaps because many of them tend to see things in the short term (usually in two to four year intervals), public officials have largely ignored the study of success and failure in the real world.

Although public policy decision makers must consider the technical, administrative, and political impact of every option under consideration, they seldom think about the *long term* implications of their decisions, and their effect on the constituents they represent and serve. They typically are inclined to make important decisions based upon the most immediate favorable political outcome. This shortsightedness has characterized much of public management and planning in the United States for the past 100-plus years. It therefore has no place in contemporary public administration.

PURPOSE OF THE BOOK

The scenarios ("brainteasers") can be used to supplement a course of study in public administration as an individual or team project, or for classroom discussion. They provide the reader an opportunity to work through a simulated real world problem. They may also assist the user in the study and preparation for a written or oral examination, or job interview that might likely contain a scenario similar to one presented in this book. Although such exercises are used by the military and emergency responders as table top exercises (the "what ifs" of planning), few opportunities present themselves for students to think of alternative solutions and their ramifications prior to being faced with the issue in the real world. In the academic setting, problems are generally addressed from the theoretical framework and lack a connection with the practical implications of the issues and potential solutions.

The scenarios contain issues such as multiple and oftentimes competing agendas, budget constraints, and the invariable organizational behavior concerns that influence morale and performance, all of which must be contemplated in the formulation of a stratagem. Each scenario provides the reader with a chance to develop a resolution strategy that will serve the needs of the people for the long term. There is more.

A community's history, its traditions and values, the quality of life in its neighborhoods, and public standards and expectations for each also must be given the fullest attention by elected and appointed public officials and public executives. These important characteristics of any community cannot be overlooked.

The reader thus becomes the centerpiece of each scenario. He or she is charged with the responsibility of successfully and effectively resolving the issue that is being presented. The user is obliged to muster his or her analytical and critical thinking skills, and unleash individual ingenuity and creativity. Remember, there is no place in contemporary public administration for shortsightedness.

HOW TO USE THE BOOK

How to analyze and solve public policy issues is something that can be learned, and learning to analyze a scenario is a giant step in that direction. An important output of a scenario is a set of recommendations for action. In the furtherance of that objective, scenarios develop diagnostic skills that provide an opportunity to solve complicated public policy issues.

For each scenario studied, students will undertake a specific role with the objective of bringing order to the various and sundry concerns in each situation. The ultimate outcome would include: 1) determining the major problem(s); 2) providing recommendations that improve or resolve the state of affairs that exists; and 3) communicating the results of the task undertaken. At first, the reader may be intimidated by the mass of facts, data, opinions, and events, as well as the politics and personalities that confront a public executive. It is important to note that the public manager can learn to address such large problems so the reader should be neither discouraged nor worried. Read the scenario carefully in order to get an appreciation of the general situation.

Next, read it with more deliberation and make notes. Obtain and understand the facts, and conduct an evaluation.

After a few exercises, the reader will be more comfortable and confident in his or her ability to solve the "mysteries." In time, the reader may develop his or her own unique approach to analyzing scenarios. In the meantime, the process must be methodical and systematic. Listed below are some decision-making models that can be utilized by the reader to start the process. The reader may want to refer to these models while working through each narrative.

Decision Making Model 1

- What is going on in a particular situation? (i.e., What is the scope of the problem?)
- Why did it happen this way?
- What are the key issues that must be resolved?
- What are the hard (quantifiable) and soft (qualitative) issues?
- What should be done next?
- What are the available alternatives?
- What outcomes should be expected from each alternative? and
- What is the best alternative?

Decision Making Model 2

- Clearly define the problem or problems (Primary and secondary issues);
- Gather the necessary information;
- Interpret the information;
- Develop solutions;
- Select the best practical solution;
- Put the solution into operation;
- Evaluate the effectiveness of the solution; and
- If necessary, select another alternative and evaluate its effectiveness

Decision Making Model 3

- Problem awareness (You can't solve a problem unless you know what it is!);
- Problem identification;
- Development of alternatives;
- Selection of best alternative;
- Implementation stage; and
- Criteria to measure success

The aforementioned models can be summarized in the basic five-step method:

- What is the problem?
- Why is it a problem?
- What are some of the possible solutions?
- What is the best solution? and
- How can the best solution be implemented and evaluated?

Decision Making Model 4

The late Wallace S. Sayre, Eaton Professor of Public Administration at Columbia University, developed a decision model that identifies nine sets of actors or power structures in the decision making process (Held, 1979). Although the Sayre Wheel model was originally designed for federal government programs, it can be modified for use at the municipal, county, and state government levels.

The Sayre Wheel displays the relationships and interplay between the principle interests that must be considered in the formulation, adoption, and implementation of policies and programs.

Decision makers must consider the ABCs of politics—alliance building, bargaining, and compromise—when analyzing the multiple power structures and their interactions.

In addition to the direct outcomes that result from a solution, it is important to remember that there frequently are unintended results. For example, a state may upgrade a road to provide for the future traffic needs, but as a result of the new upgrades, there is increased construction and population growth. The road is a catalyst of growth, although that was not the intent at the time. It is important to consider the "Law of the Unintended Consequence" in each scenario.

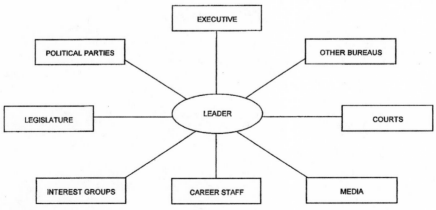

Figure 1.   Sayre Wheel Model

Introduction

There is an ever increasing need for individuals to increase their competencies so that such competencies match what is needed in the workplace of the future. In *The Bases of Competence: Skills for Lifelong Learning and Employability* (1998), Evers, Rush, and Berdrow indicate skills required for the future are not taught in college but are developed. Schools reward good communication skills by getting good grades. The students, on the other hand, also learn how to get things done, how to manage their time in order to get their assignments and tasks completed, how to communicate, and other personal and interpersonal skills. In their article on "The base of Competence: Skill Development during the Transition from University to Work," Evers and Rush categorized these competencies into four broad areas: mobilizing innovation and change; managing people and tasks; communicating; and managing self (1996, 280–281).

Individuals need to be able to conceptualize. This involves obtaining pertinent information that can come from various sources and analyzing the information in terms of the issue at hand. Once analyzed, the information is synthesized to address the new or different context. The situations may require an innovative solution, something that is different than the norm. When information is thus applied to a new situation, there is a degree of risk that must be addressed. Risk can be classified as reasonable when it is considered reasonable. That is accomplished when an assessment of different ways of meeting the objective, denoted as the alternatives to the issue. With each alternative, there are potentially positive and negative outcomes that need to be assessed in order to assess the degree of risk associated with each alternative.

Managing people and tasks involves the basic functions of planning, organizing, staffing, delegating, coordinating, organizing, reporting, and budgeting. These tasks and functions require timely decision-making. Decisions are made with recognition of long and short term effects of the potential solution. The values of the individual and/or the organization impact on the decision-making process as does the political climate in which such decision is made. The business environment frequently demands more large-scale changes through new strategies, reengineering, mergers, acquisitions, downsizing, new market or new product development, and other such activities. The changing environment affects organizational and individual decisions. The issues become larger and more complex. In addition, the issues are more emotionally charged. Decisions must be made more quickly even though the environment is less certain. There is also the need for those implementing the decisions to sacrifice more in order for the changes to take place. Changing the decision making process may be needed for a number of reasons. As operations become more complex, there is no single person who has all the information needed to make all the major decisions. In some cases, there is too much information available; while in other situations, there may be information but it is neither readily available nor easily understood. An additional problem may be that a single person does not have the time and credibility that is needed to convince the number of people needed to implement the decisions made. In this process, conflict resolution and negotiation may be supplementary skills needed to ensure the best decision is selected.

Communication competencies include verbal and written forms as well as the non-verbal modes. In interpersonal relationships, individuals not only hear the words and the message, but they interpret how the sender of the message feels through body language or tone. An important part of the process is listening to the message and responding appropriately to what is being said. Written communications takes various forms. It can be a formal report, a formal or informal memorandum, or even an email. Although the more formal written communications allow writers the opportunity to clarify and refine their thoughts and ensure the message is clearly articulated, an important factor since the reader will not see the non-verbal cues that accompany in person communications, the move to email and instant messaging has resulted in the transmission of poorly written and incomplete messages. Such actions can send the wrong message to the reader. Care must be taken to send a message that is free from grammatical errors and open to interpretation.

Managing self involves learning and developing personal strengths as well as problem solving and analytic thinking. Such competencies require individuals to continue to learn, the lifelong learning movement that has become more operational as significant changes are impacting the workplace. Problem solving and analytic thinking involves identifying, prioritizing, and solving problems. How this is accomplished is asking the right questions to solicit essential information as well as providing ideas and suggestions from an individual's point of view. The manner in which problems are solved can be along a continuum from the rational type of analysis where the solutions is based on historical data and information and the analysis is conducted in terms that are familiar to the individual or group solving the problem to the creative process where alternatives may not be those with which the organization has a history or of which it has specific knowledge. The creative approach involves "thinking outside the box," which is difficult for many in the public sector who are in regimented operational areas.

Critical thinking is related to engaging students with a problem. It is sometimes difficult to have students look at the various problems that exist around them. Individuals frequently encounter practical issues and not merely exercises that address a specific academic problem. Critical thinking and learning can be linked with writing. As individuals work through the problem solving process, evaluate alternatives, and determine a solution, many write the various components of the process. The end result is generally a written report.

The exercises included in this book require critical thinking skills and should include a written report or summary of the process and response. The various components of the final product include the problem solving/decision making process as well as a written report that is technically grammatically correct. The purpose is to provide opportunities for students to improve their communication skills, which is improving one's self. As the individual develops critical thinking skills and one's own self, there may be an expansion of alternatives for any one of the scenarios. Conversely, the less experienced and/or learned an individual is, the more limited the number of alternatives considered. Throughout the development process, then, the exercises may result in different results based on the individual(s) involved.

PREVIOUS EXPERIENCE

There are times when the public manager faces issues that have occurred in the past. Although the tendency of the public manager is to look at what happened in the past and what worked and what did not work, there may have been significant changes in the environment that make such retrospection inappropriate. Generally, the forces and trends that impact operational factors are classified as political, economic, social, environmental, legal, and technological in scope, although there may be additional factors that will impact the new decision. For example, educational trends are important for colleges and universities, but they will also impact other areas since higher levels of education for members of a specific workforce may result in the individuals challenging decisions. In addition, a more highly educated workforce may bring new ideas based on their experience and their own biases. Globalization and its influences form another major trend. Although many in the public sector argue that globalization only has a small direct impact on the public sector, it is a larger impact than many want to admit. Cultural values and norms, diversity, immigration, and many other factors are tied to the global view and are an influence on the public and not-for-profit sectors as well as in the private sector. Public administrators need to remain current of these and other current forces and trends as they impact what services are provided and how individuals do their jobs.

Decisions must be made, but there are times when the individuals who are given this task lack the necessary information to make the most effective or efficient decision. The decision process may require the use of a team or workgroup where the individual members bring specific expertise to the process. The scenarios can be used in this type of setting. The more scenarios the student addresses, the more competencies that are developed.

LEGAL DISCLAIMER

Although certain scenarios may be based on actual events, the situations, places, and persons are creations of the authors. Any person, place, or situation depicted in these scenarios is fictitious. No location, circumstance, or person, living or dead, is intended or should be inferred.

SCENARIOS

One

The Maginot Line Theory: Using Old Solutions to Solve New Problems

Historically, the Department of Public Works has enjoyed a favorable reputation among the people who live and work in the city. It is recognized as an efficient organization that thoroughly accomplishes its mission. Because the general public acknowledges a relatively high approval rating through municipal surveys conducted from time to time, its standing in the community is an obvious benefit to local government administrators due to its cost effectiveness, productivity, and positive political consequences.

The department has a diverse workforce that consists of employees with a wide range of time-in-service experience. Group cohesiveness, the psychological cement that bonds the group together, is considered exceptional. The morale of the workforce is considered to be high, and people generally interact very well with one another, both among themselves and with department supervisors and administrators. Conformity with established standards and practices are enforced through peer group influence.

Within the workforce, however, are a few cliques that reflect the values, attitudes, and beliefs of participating employees, particularly with regard to labor-management relations. The largest of the peer groups consists of a majority of employees with overlapping agendas. The group's informal leader is a veteran employee with twenty-one years of experience. He is highly respected by the workers and acknowledged as the one person who always looks out for their interests, both individually and collectively. Whenever there is an issue to be resolved, the employees typically look to him for guidance. He frequently intervenes on their behalf and is able to resolve most grievances between labor and management without the need for union intervention. This process, albeit informal, is of great benefit to both the administration and the workforce. Because of these successes, as a matter of custom and practice, employees almost never reach out for a management representative whenever a labor issue arises. A substantial majority of department employees are comfortable and satisfied with this process. Many of the newer employees, however, believe that procedures for dealing with labor-management matters should be formalized and not left to an informal leader with the "power" to arbitrarily decide what he thinks are the appropriate ways and means of resolving a particular issue in question. Furthermore, the informal group leader has indicated his intention to retire in a year or two making formal procedures an organizational imperative.

One of the peer group members was recently promoted within the department. Although he has less than ten years of experience, he is respected by most employees and regarded as qualified, competent, and sensitive to workforce labor concerns. His job description includes both operational and administrative authority over many of the same employees with whom he had been working for several years. Most employees look upon his promotion as being good for the organization as well as good for them since this individual has worked his way up and brings with him knowledge of how the operations really work.

One of his first acts was to issue a set of directives that, in effect, orders absolute adherence to the organization's formal chain-of-command. The directives imply that failure to comply will lead to disciplinary action against the offending member. Although well intended, the rigid discipline imposed on the informal organization immediately created morale problems among most members of the workforce. The informal group's peer leader felt as though the new procedures were an attempt to usurp or subvert his traditional leadership role within the organization. He considered their implementation a sign of disrespect for his longevity and faithful years of service to the department. Most of the employees felt the same as their peer group leader. Almost immediately, absenteeism increased along with reported job related injuries. Overtime was on the increase as a result. Not long thereafter, productivity markedly diminished and public support began to noticeably decline. Soon, public officials were feeling the political effects of the labor unrest.

The Director of Public Works is confronted with a two-headed monster. Does she support her manager's effort to formally change the organization's culture, which in the long-term will benefit the department and its employees? Does she reverse the order and thus restore the group cohesiveness that previously existed? If she selects the latter decision option, how will this affect her supervisory staff's morale and the execution of their duties and responsibilities within the organization? If she lets the directive stand, what further fallout can she anticipate?

As a member of the management team at the Department of Public Works, you are called by the director and asked to assess the scope of the problem and develop a strategy to resolve the issue to the satisfaction of both management and labor, while concomitantly mitigating the political consequences for the Mayor and members of city council.

Assignment: You are to develop a report to the Director of Public Works that provides the scope of the problem as well as a recommendation on how to address the issue(s).

Two

Seniority versus Education: Resurrection of an Old Debate

The city administration is currently in the process of reviewing criteria for promotional consideration for personnel employed in its various operating departments. The process has virtually divided the eight-member study team into three sub-groups. One sub-group strongly believes that time-in-service is a necessary qualifier for advancement and should be assigned greater weight than any other consideration. After all, is there really any substitute for on-the-job experience? A second sub-group insists that every other qualifier should be subordinate to education as a selection criterion. Its reasoning is quite simple: the modern, dynamic, high-tech contemporary organization cannot accomplish its mission without an educated workforce. Therefore, an individual's education and training must necessarily transcend experience as a primary promotional consideration. A third sub-group argues that, while experience and education are undeniably important considerations, other factors must be included in a list of qualifiers, such as attendance records, physical and psychological fitness, disciplinary history, and the number and type of laudatory correspondence, commendations, and awards received. This small sub-group believes that factors such as those indicated give a manager far more insight into a person's qualification for promotion than either experience or education considered separately. The attitude of this group's members is grounded on the belief that experience and education matter little by themselves. Rather, they should be measured alongside several other criterions to ensure the best qualified candidate is selected for promotion.

Neither of the sub-groups has even reconciled the issue of whether or not written and oral examinations are necessary and appropriate to the selection process. Some team participants believe that examinations indicate nothing more than a candidate's ability to memorize information, which frequently results in the promotion of the best test taker and not the best candidate for the job. Others judge that exams are necessary, not only as a measuring device but as safeguard against the potential for human bias compromising the selection process.

The discussion appears to have reached a stalemate concerning all issues under deliberation, including the weighted percentages of each of the factors under consideration. The study team has summoned you to the discussions. They want detailed input from someone in the workforce who can see the issue from an entirely different perspective. Your constructive contribution will be greatly valued, and your association will enhance the reliability of the process, as well as the credibility of the study team.

After much careful thought, you begin to formalize the presentation that you will deliver before the study team. How well you articulate and defend your recommendations will do much to break the deadlock. A consensus will most certainly be reached that will have a significant and lasting impact on the future of the organization. What are your recommendations? How did you make that determination? What pertinent facts can you use to support your position?

Three

EAP Referral: Overreaction or Organizational Necessity?

In your position as an assistant comptroller in a municipal tax collector's office, you have oversight responsibility for a staff of eight employees; only one of whom (we shall call him Andrew) is authorized to process cash transactions. Cash transactions include daily deposits at a local bank. Andrew has been a reliable employee with an unblemished record for seven years. His loyalty and integrity are without question. He is considered a reliable and valuable employee. In the office, he is generally sociable and upbeat. He is not only well-liked, but highly respected as well. Andrew is regarded as a serious, consummate professional by his peers and supervisors when it comes to the performance of the duties and responsibilities of his position. In short, his gregarious personality contributes to the office staff's high morale, and his work history has been exemplary.

In the past two weeks, however, there has been a noticeable change in Andrew's behavior. Although his work performance has remained consistent, his demeanor in the office has not. Lately, he has been quiet and somewhat withdrawn. There has been some speculation among office staffers as to the reason. One unconfirmed rumor alleges marital problems between Andrew and his spouse over personal financial management issues at home. The source of the rumor is reported to be a male co-worker. The co-worker and Andrew began working in the tax collector's office together seven years ago on the same date. Everyone in the office is aware of their close personal relationship, which adds credibility to the story.

Since you are a friend and professional colleague and are sincerely concerned about Andrew's state of mind, you invite him to lunch with the intent to raise the issue of the obvious change in his personality at the office. You decide, however, that asking him about rumored marital problems would be inappropriate. As the discussion proceeds, Andrew acknowledges the change in his persona and voluntarily confirms having some personal problems at home. Andrew further admits that the difficulties at home have been competing with his ability to concentrate on his duties at work. Nothing more is revealed during the luncheon.

It becomes obvious to you that Andrew's commitment at work is competing with a variety of other issues; a condition known as partial inclusion. Since Andrew's work product remains satisfactory, you decide to continue to observe his conduct in the office before deciding on a course of action, should one become necessary.

At the conclusion of the work day, you and Andrew coincidentally leave city hall together. As you reach the parking lot, Andrew confides in you that he has incurred a substantial debt during a series of recent visits to gambling casinos in the region. As a result, he is overdue on mortgage and car payments, and has been delinquent in paying his home maintenance expenses in the past few months. Andrew insists he will be able to overcome this difficulty by means of more deliberate and thoughtful money management of his personal finances. Andrew also indicates he and his wife have been arguing incessantly over the circumstances of the incurred debt and the obvious consequences resulting from their financial difficulties. Nevertheless, Andrew assures you that he will be able to work things out and recover from the debt. He promises that his problem will not become your problem. He thanks you for listening and asks you to consider his personal problems in the strictest of confidence.

During the drive home, many thoughts go through your mind regarding Andrew's personal affairs. One of the things you don't wish to do is compromise your relationship with him by revealing the information you learned to your immediate superior, the city's Chief Financial Office. Further, you do not believe there are legitimate grounds at this interval to refer Andrew to the city's Employee Assistance Program counselor, either voluntarily or by forced compliance. After all, there were no witnesses to the lunchtime or after work conversations. Andrew may very well change his story substantively or possibly deny it entirely if officially challenged.

On the drive to work the next day your thoughts about the matter begin to change remarkably. You are concerned that there are a set of risks associated with revealing Andrew's personal problems to the Chief Financial Officer. You do not want to expose him to ridicule and embarrassment. Certainly, you do not want to lose him as an employee and friend. Then again, there are potential equal or greater risks of keeping his personal problems confidential. You decide to do two things immediately. First, you will carefully consider both options and their likely consequences (both for yourself as well as the organization) should you elect act on one or the other. Next, you must be prepared to articulate your thoughts judiciously before the Chief Financial Officer if that is the most likely choice of action, and be ready to recommend and defend your proposed course of action. There is no time to procrastinate.

Assignment: Given the facts at hand, what steps would you take to address this issue? What liabilities are there if you do nothing? In your view, is there a problem with his handling the cash transactions?

Four

The Police Matrix: Toward a More Efficient Division of Labor

Congratulations! After twelve years of service in the department's Patrol Division, you have been promoted to sergeant on a one-year probationary basis and assigned to the Administrative Division/Planning and Research Unit. It is your dream job—a chance to unleash your creative juices. It is also gratifying to know you are the department's first female to occupy the position. There is much to do. The 75-member agency has not yet reached its projected full capacity, and the city is still growing, although the growth has slowed somewhat in recent years.

You begin to compile a "to do" list to help guide you through the first few months in your new challenging and exciting job responsibilities. At the outset, all seems to be going well. The Chief of Police has offered his vision of what the department should look like in the coming years. He has presented you with a series of goals and objectives that you are eager to begin working to accomplish. A few weeks have passed since your promotion and reassignment. The members and employees of the department are confident that you will be successful throughout your assignment in the Planning and Research Unit. They are looking forward to a sample of things to come from your office.

The timing of your elevation in rank and reassignment coincides with the end of the city's fiscal year. At the next regularly scheduled weekly police department staff meeting, the Chief of Police lamentably announces that the city's revenue projections indicate that there will be a significant budget deficit and corresponding debt in the next fiscal year. The Chief alerts the members of his staff that the mayor recently indicated he will ask the city council to authorize a contract for the services of an independent study team to review the city's operating units and make general recommendations for improving service delivery at a substantially reduced cost. The study team is based at a nearby prestigious university. Certainly, the team's distinguished reputation will ensure that most, if not all, of their recommendations will be implemented. It would be virtual political suicide for the mayor and council to ignore its recommendations and continue to operate with a mounting debt. The Chief asks all members and employees to cooperate with the study team's review of the police department. Concurrently, the Chief immediately orders the suspension of all spending not associated with operating expenses. Your office is ordered to stand-down on all activity where the allocation of public funds is involved. Your excitement has turned to frustration. You nervously and anxiously await the recommendations of the study team.

Three months after being awarded the contract to review the city's departments, the study team releases its report to the mayor and council. Although it contains a set of general recommendations, it leaves specific decision-making to the various department heads as to how each recommendation is acted upon. The police department section of the report indicates that the agency's table of organization is top-heavy, and contains unnecessary and costly overlaps. (See Figure 2). Recommendations also include eliminating certain non-critical sub-units. Because these units are available on an as-needed basis from the county sheriff's office, they are considered wasteful and an unnecessary duplication of effort. These units include the department's crime laboratory, canine teams, telecommunications unit, and the drug enforcement spe-

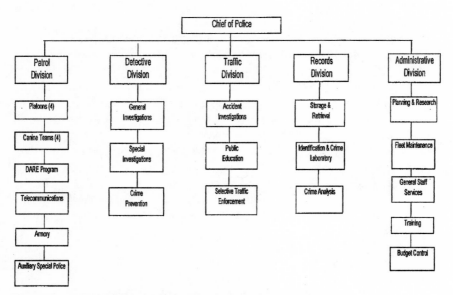

Figure 2.   Police Department Divisions Currently Under Review

cial investigations squad. The Chief instructs you to review the study team's report and furnish him with a set of specific cost-cutting recommendations.

After the department's members and employees have the opportunity to read the entire study team's report, the consequences are immediate and considerable. The union representing the 75 sworn members files a grievance on the basis that certain ranks will be eliminated that are "guaranteed" by the collective bargaining agreement between the city and the police union. The membership further argues that the elimination of the canine teams and/or the telecommunications unit represent a clear and present danger to police officer safety. In addition, assignment to the drug enforcement special investigative unit has always been considered a preferred duty assignment that is both interesting and rewarding. The department's best performers have been traditionally utilized in this unit, and over the years, several members have received promotions after serving there. The department has an excellent reputation in the community and among law enforcement agencies for its drug control initiatives. It is a source of pride among department members. When community leaders hear of its proposed elimination, they too strenuously object.

To you, it seems as though everything is unraveling. What is more, for reasons you can't understand, many of the rank and file members are blaming you for the "morale busting" list of study team recommendations currently under review. You are perceived as the catalyst for everything that is going wrong since they are occurring simultaneous with your assignment to Planning and Research.

Nevertheless, the Chief awaits your report. How do you help him successfully implement the needed changes while at the same time not blocking opportunities for individual growth and development? How can you help him reconcile the city's demand to cut costs with the police union's apparent unwavering argument on the subject of guaranteed staffing levels, and police officer safety concerns? What about the critical issue of morale and its influence on performance? How will all of this affect you personally, both individually and as a career law enforcement officer?

As you consider the organizational chart and staffing pattern, you consider reshaping the matrix. The divisions that appear in the above table of organization are commanded by lieutenants (5), at least three of whom are approaching eligibility for retirement. For the purpose of this exercise, each lieutenant earns an annual salary of $65,000 plus a benefit package in the amount of 15%. Therefore, the total cost to staff each division by one lieutenant is $74,750. Each sub-division or unit is commanded by one sergeant (23), each earning $58,000 annually with a 15% benefit package.

Seven sergeants are currently eligible for retirement. The total cost to staff each sub-division by one sergeant is $66,700.

The mayor has pledged there will be no layoffs within the police department, although there will, however, be a hiring freeze during the next fiscal year, and perhaps beyond. Assume that current staffing levels at the police officer position will remain static at 47, although nine police officers are eligible for retirement during the next fiscal year. Without using exact numbers of personnel, where/when should the remaining members be deployed?

Five

To Approve or Disapprove? That Is the Question

You and your colleague Victor are employed as code enforcement officers for the Borough of Grasswick, a small, one square mile village with a total population of 5,200 people, consisting mainly of middle and upper class residents. You have been a full-time employee of the borough working your entire career of eighteen years in its Building Inspections Office. Victor is a part-time employee who began working for the borough less than one year ago. Victor also works for his father's packaging company, a small business located in a town about ten miles from Grasswick. Victor's family business has no contracts with the borough. As a matter of fact, they rarely make a customer service delivery in the municipality. Since you plan to retire in two years and relocate to Arizona, it has been your responsibility to train Victor as a code enforcement official and prepare him to assume your full-time duties and responsibilities upon your retirement.

During the lunch break each day of the work week, you and Victor, as well as other public executives from the borough, enjoy a meal at Downey's Restaurant across the street from the Grasswick Borough Hall. There are two other luncheonette-type establishments within walking distance from the hall whose ownership changes from time to time. Conversely, Downey's has been a family-owned and operated institution in the borough for sixty years. Its location is convenient and thus allows for more real time to enjoy an afternoon lunch. Furthermore, the food is consistently enjoyable, and the service staff is both friendly and responsive. It is a place where everyone knows one another on a first-name basis. Downey's Restaurant is a one-story attached building situated in a row of commercial establishments on Main Street. It is open for business from 7:30 A.M. until 9:00 P.M. The Downey family would like to change its closing time to midnight to attract patrons of a recently opened

15

multiplex movie theatre located one-half mile outside of the borough limits on a state highway.

When you and Victor arrive at the Building Inspection Office the next morning, the borough's chief building inspector advises you that the Downey family has agreed to purchase an adjoining store front property contingent upon the approval of a variance application. The application requests that the borough issue the requisite permits that will make restaurant expansion possible. The Downey's seek permission to break through the wall of the adjoining property and increase the seating capacity of the restaurant. In doing so, they would expand their hours of operation to hopefully attract the theatre patrons. The Downey's argue that the proposal is good for both the ownership and the borough. The family has inferred they may construct a new building in a contiguous municipality if the application is rejected. If they do so, the borough will lose a historic community landmark as well as an important ratable.

Once the request for the variance becomes a matter of public record, owners of the two other luncheonettes on Main Street immediately apply for a variance that will allow them to increase their hours of operation to midnight as well. They too want to attract patrons of the multiplex theatre. In the succeeding weeks, additional merchants along Main Street begin to apply for similar variances for the same purpose. They reason that theatre patrons, looking for a place to eat before or after viewing a movie, may also patronize their individual stores as well.

At the outset, the borough council has indicated it will support the applications once they are reviewed and approved by the Building Inspection Office. Council members believe that the approvals would be good for business in the borough. Some members infer that they expect the Building Inspection Office to approve all of the applications for extended hours as well as Downey's request to expand its restaurant. Council members know that it is very important for the applications to be approved for political reasons. Business owners live in the town, and their families, friends, and patrons vote. Successful commercial enterprises are also the life blood of any municipality. Their vitality lessens the likelihood of tax increases for homeowners. Rejection of any application may mean the difference between being reelected and turned out of office.

Meanwhile, a political firestorm is brewing among the borough's civic leaders. Since many homes are located on streets parallel to Main Street, residents are objecting to any expansion of the operating hours along the commercial corridor. They are concerned with vehicular and pedestrian traffic, noise, and disorderly conduct (since most theatre-goers tend to be teenagers).

The residents want to maintain the borough's peace and tranquility and its small-town image. They want the sidewalks rolled up by 9:00 P.M.

The borough council is sitting on the horns of a political dilemma; so are you. If you recommend the original building expansion proposal submitted by the Downey family, you lock in a closing time of midnight for its restaurant operations. Nevertheless, you are prepared to affirm the variance request for Downey's and forward it to the chief building inspector. Applications received from other commercial property owners have not as yet been formally considered. You know that approval of the Downey application will open the proverbial can of worms. Other commercial property owners most certainly will object to the Downey expansion if their variance applications are subsequently denied.

You know that the borough council is certainly hypersensitive to the commercial-residential-political issues that will certainly cascade from any decision that is made. In the final analysis, it will likely result in a win-lose situation for all of the interests involved. If the Downey application is approved and the other petitions rejected, the local newspaper has advised the mayor and council that it is prepared to print a series of articles dealing with the entire controversy. The exposé will begin with an editorial questioning the ethics of the borough administration for favoring the Downey application over all of the others. It will infer that there has been on ongoing relationship for at least two decades between Downey family members and borough officials who have patronized their restaurant.

The implication is obvious. Since you are the first person in the application review process, your personal integrity will be subject to suspicion if you decide to approve the Downey application and disapprove all of the others. Since business owners and residents are up in arms over the entire matter, the borough council has requested an impact study as to the likely consequences of any decision you will make with regard to any and all of the variance applications. The chief building inspector directs you to prepare the report and attach it to your recommendation(s). He insists that you also reconcile the question of ethics and include the subject as an addendum to the report to be presented to the borough council.

Since you can apply for early retirement and virtually avoid the controversies in their entirety, why not do it and move to Arizona a couple of years earlier than you anticipated? Your decision(s) please.

Six

A Performance Appraisal Process: Form over Function?

Working six years for Department of Human Services, a state agency in a largely rural section of the state, has been a reasonably enjoyable experience for you. Most everyone enjoys working for the organization. There are no pressures; few, if any, employee-management issues ever arise; overall working conditions are favorable; the facility is neat, clean, and safe; and salaries are considered to be very good. Although opportunities for upward mobility are limited due to the relatively small size of the workforce (55), you are being considered for a promotion to section supervisor. If you receive the advancement, you will have oversight responsibility for eight employees who perform repetitive, practically assembly line-type job tasks. It is known as the Client Services Contact Section.

Each employee of the Client Services Contact Section makes telephone contact with at-risk teenage men and women. Each client is surveyed on a number of human relation factors. Afterward, the survey reports are forwarded to the section supervisor for review. If there are any "red flag" indicators detected on a report, a department field counselor is directed to make personal, in-home contact with the at-risk individual. Although the new job will not be particularly exciting or stimulating, you look forward to the new challenge.

During the previous four-year period, the number of client contacts has remained constant while the number of clients has increased by 20%. If you are fortunate enough to somehow increase the unit's productivity, there is a possibility that you might be considered for a promotion to division supervisor some day. Other than working on the commissioner's staff, division supervisor is considered to be a somewhat prestigious title.

What is more, one division supervisor has notified the department that she is considering a lateral transfer to another state agency. She is likely to reach a decision within the next month, and thereafter submit her transfer paperwork. If she follows through with her intention to leave Department of Human Services, her departure will result in a division supervisor's vacancy.

The following Friday afternoon you are summoned to the deputy commissioner's office and told you have been promoted to section supervisor. You are instructed to report for a brief training regimen beginning Monday morning. Soon, you will begin supervising the Client Services Contact Section.

Not long after beginning your new job responsibilities, it becomes obvious that there isn't much you can do to motivate the eight employees under your supervision. You offer your encouragement and support; you are considerate and friendly, and the group both likes and respects you. After a period of several weeks, however, there has been no spike in their productivity. You are under no pressure from agency executives to increase the group's output. As a matter of fact, the real purpose for any initiative to increase productivity in the Client Services Contact Section is purely self-serving; to bring positive attention to yourself in order to be considered for a promotion in the future. Your workgroup doesn't know this, nor would they care very much even if they did.

Your curiosity about the maintenance of their performance effort causes you to ask the section's senior member to informally account for the apparent indifference. You learn a few things that you never considered to be of any importance throughout the course of your employment with the agency. Your senior employee tells you that the group is comfortable with production that is constant. If the group increases production in a given period, the agency will likely insist it maintain the increase. If they underachieve, they may not only be criticized, but each section member may be issued an unsatisfactory performance appraisal as well. Simply stated, the group practices performance avoidance. They like the stability and the psychological safety associated with unvarying "production" numbers.

Every employee of Department of Human Services receives a written annual performance appraisal prepared by his/her immediate supervisor. The forms are delivered to each employee in an envelope marked, "CONFIDENTIAL" on December 31st of each year. The appraisal system is designed to measure individual achievement against the basic standards of each job description. Since job descriptions and the corresponding standards are published, there is no mystery as to what is expected from each agency employee. Individual performance is either satisfactory or unsatisfactory. If unsatisfactory, the reasons are indicated in the space marked "Needs Improvement" on the appraisal form. If a person receives two or more unsatisfactory performance appraisals within a five-year period, he or she may be subject to disciplinary action. However, it is a rare occurrence when an employee receives even one unsatisfactory appraisal during the indicated period. This is not because supervisors are so-called high markers, nor is it because supervisors do not wish to cause disharmony within the workforce. Employees simply do exactly what they are expected to do.

So far as you know, this system has historically worked well in the Department of Human Services. You have no personal complaint about the process. Nevertheless, you silently question the reason the performance review process isn't working the way it should. You ask yourself how the process can be improved. If you are promoted to division supervisor one day, would it not be to your benefit if incentives were established at the earliest opportunity to increase overall agency productivity? You are thinking about proposing a strategic plan to the Commissioner's office. If implemented, it will most likely increase productivity. A substantial portion of the proposal concerns the overhaul of the performance appraisal process.

You still have mixed emotions about doing anything, however. Everything seems to running smoothly, and people enjoy a high level of job satisfaction. Any action that upsets the norm may result in significant consequences in the short term for both yourself and the organization. Conversely, to do nothing may actually cause harm to both yourself and the agency over the long term, after all there has been talk about privatization or the restructuring of the organization through consolidation of titles and functions. You must think beyond your emotions. What should you do?

Seven

Job Satisfaction: In the Eye of the Beholder

You have been recently named the city's Administrative Staff Services Director. The staff you supervise consists of a workforce of 28 men and women assigned to perform a variety of clerical and secretarial functions for most of the city's departments. (The fire and police department's have their own separate support staffs.) The workgroup is situated in a large, second floor office in the city hall building. You can easily supervise the entire group literally from your office in same work area.

The Staff Services Department workgroup is separated into the following functional components, along with the corresponding number of employees assigned to each task:

Management Information Systems: Data entry/retrieval (5)
Telephone Operators: Public information and call referrals (5)
Clerical: Word processing (7)
Messenger Services: (2)
Public Reception/Information: (2)
Secretarial Pool: City department secretaries (7)

Fifteen of the employees have worked for the city for 20 years or longer (63%); seven from between 10 and 15 years (20%); and the remaining six (17%), for less than ten years, two of whom have less than two years of experience. The most senior employees tend to migrate over time to the Secretarial Pool, because it is considered the most prestigious assignment in the Administrative Staff Services Department. Salary is determined by longevity, not by assigned task.

The current department was established over forty years ago and has changed very little since its inception. The most significant changes have been associated with the introduction of new technologies. Typewriters, cabinet files, and adding machines have passed into history. With regard to personnel management, almost nothing has changed. Historically, when a vacancy is created as a result of a transfer (a rare occurrence) or retirement, a new-hire typically is assigned to the vacated position. The person is trained for that position and assigned thereto throughout the length of their employment with the city. There is almost no turnover of personnel in the Administrative Staff Services Department.

Although you are new to this particular department, you have been working for the city for nine years and understand the importance of each function of the Administrative Staff Services Department. In your prior assignment as Deputy Director of Public Works, you utilized its services on a daily basis. Not only are you familiar with its operation, you also know all of the individuals assigned to staff services on a first-name basis. So far as you know, there are no outstanding labor-management issues that need to be rectified.

Two of the employees, Linda and Bill, have worked for the city for 12 years, both having entered public service during the technology revolution of the 1990s. They have been assigned to the Administrative Staff Services Department for most of their respective careers, and are accustomed to its culture and tradition. Like most others in the workgroup, Linda and Bill had to adjust to the introduction of new technologies. Although the duties, responsibilities, and performance expectations of the group have not changed very much, the way in which they are executed has changed considerably. Hi-tech work stations have made each job function resemble a virtual assembly line, each with an interchangeable human part. Linda and Bill have different views on how the workgroup should operate. Linda wants to use the "interchangeable parts" argument to transform the way things are done. Conversely, Bill prefers leaving well enough alone.

If you were a fly on the wall, you would overhear the following conversation between the two advocates:

LINDA: "I am presently enrolled in a personnel administration course at the university. One of the topics is job satisfaction. I learned that a way to eliminate boredom on the job is to cross-train the workgroup to perform each task assigned to staff services. Wouldn't that make coming to work more interesting if group members could be assigned to different sub-units from time to time?"

BILL: "Why do that? Every person in the group is happy with his or her respective job assignment, and each is very good at what they do. Why would you want to tamper with a good thing? Haven't you heard the old axiom, 'If it ain't broke, don't fix it'?"

LINDA: "I'm not so sure they are all happy, nor am I certain that it ain't broke. Invariably, every time someone is on sick leave or takes a vacation some other person has to perform the tasks of the vacated position. That is when you hear the griping about 'unfamiliarity'."

BILL: "My point exactly. If that is the case, why change *everyone* for the sake of change when even temporary changes cause problems?"

LINDA: "There is more to it than that. It is inevitable that there are going to be a substantial number of retirements in the next several years. Do you really expect people coming off the street to immediately fill those positions and perform at the same level of excellence to which the city is accustomed?"

BILL: "Why not? It has worked so far."

LINDA: "You're begging the question."

BILL: "I don't think it is necessary to rock the proverbial boat. It seems to me to be much ado about nothing."

LINDA: "Think of it this way. By cross-training everyone, the department will really have interchangeable parts. No matter how many vacancies occur, we can be assured the system will work to its utmost capability. We should plan ahead for this eventuality, rather than wait and be overwhelmed later."

BILL: "I'll need more than the 'vacancy' argument to accept your line of reasoning."

LINDA: "Fair point. Quite frankly, I think that job rotation is more fulfilling than coming to work each day acting as an automaton. Every person will be trained to perform all of the duties and responsibilities within the department. Overall proficiencies improve. Each person immediately becomes a more valued employee. Besides, some good ideas may come out of this. Feedback will be a reality, rather than a fantasy. Selfishly, each employee will have the ability to leverage their newly acquired skills if they decide to pursue employment elsewhere should they desire to do so. I think there is a case to be made here; the individual *and* the organization benefit."

BILL: "With all due respect, I still disagree. Few people ever leave the department. Perhaps the reason they stay here so long is because they like the safety, stability, and security of their respective job functions. Who cares about that text book stuff on the subject of job rotation? Do you really believe these people care about rewarding and challenging work? Their 'reward' is the permanence of their respective assignments. Quality of work life is in the eye of the beholder."

LINDA: "Has anyone asked them about how they really feel? Maybe one of us will be surprised to hear what they have to say. I think it's about time we leave the dinosaur age behind us once and for all. We adjusted to new technologies and we can adjust to modern personnel administration as well. Are you willing to discuss the matter with the Director if I can get an appointment with him?"

BILL: "I suppose. But I will play the devil's advocate and take an opposing point of view. I will argue that your proposal will upset the people and have an adverse impact of morale and performance."

LINDA: "Okay. Make your case. No hard feelings. Yours is an argument for the *status quo* and mine is an argument for progress—necessary change that will enhance morale and improve performance."

BILL: "If he accepts your position, you had better pray that the intended outcomes will be what you say they will be!"

Linda and Bill have formalized each argument and anxiously await their meeting with you. You listen intently as they make their respective cases point-by-point. Do you take the risk and accept Linda's position? Or do you acknowledge Bill's contention that there are no system-wide deficiencies that require overhaul within the Administrative Staff Services Department?

First, you must take the time to consider the strengths and weaknesses of each argument. Next, you must assess the likely administrative, technical, and political consequences of either decision. What is your decision?

Eight

Disciplinary Action:
Step-by-step, a Losing Process

As Director of Public Works, you question how the case was lost? How can a Judge of an Administrative Court order the reinstatement of an employee who has committed multiple and repeated violations of the organization's work rules? It just doesn't make sense. What was wrong with our case? How can an administrative court judge rule against a department-head and in favor of an employee with the unenviable record that characterized the defendant?

By way of historical commentary, when Greg was hired five years ago, he had no difficulty making it through the six-month probationary period for employees assigned to the seven-member Municipal Streets Department. It seemed as though it was the high water mark in his brief career, however. His post-probation performance has been largely unsatisfactory. His frequent absenteeism (sick leave and injury leave) and recurrent tardiness have caused road repair work projects to be postponed on several occasions. When Greg is on a work crew, he often fails to do what is expected of him. He habitually malingers and routinely takes unauthorized work breaks. Consequently, the other crew members are forced to work longer and harder in order to complete their daily assignments. Naturally, they voice their objections and dissent to their immediate supervisor.

These conditions have been contributing to highway renovation backlogs with increasing frequency. What is more, the remaining six employees have been complaining to their union shop steward that they have been ordered to work out of their respective job classifications more frequently than union members in similar sized road departments in the region. The union has threatened to take the job reassignment issue to court. Although there has been no formal job action, absenteeism, particularly due to reported work-related injuries, has increased among Greg's coworkers. Could this be the typical retaliation so often associated with perceived unfairness and inequity on the job? Is it an indication of things to come? Or could it perhaps be a warning of sort? It most certainly can be attributed to diminishing morale.

At the end of every annual evaluation period, Greg has been informed of his performance discrepancies and ordered to correct each one or face eventual disciplinary action. Greg has responded to these repeated warnings with indifference. Management decides it is time to act.

At the conclusion of the last evaluation cycle, Greg was presented with a list of accusations and formally charged with violation of several work rules. It is the first time an employee has been charged with a work-related offense in nearly 20 years. You perceive that this remedy will be appealing to the remaining employees. They most certainly will take notice that management is finally initiating corrective action concerning Greg's ongoing unsatisfactory performance record.

Having been served with the inter-departmental charges, Greg has the option of accepting summary disciplinary action, a 30-day suspension, or the alternative of having the case presented before an administrative court for adjudication. Greg decides to select the latter. Meanwhile, Greg is suspended pending the administrative hearing.

Weeks later, while you are preparing the case against Greg, you are confronted by the union representative who objects to the filing of charges. He states unequivocally that there are no grounds for charging Greg, and that the accused has the full and unwavering support of his union brothers and sisters. Further, the union has retained the services of an attorney to prepare Greg's defense. You know that if Greg is not judged guilty and suspended, the city will be charged with the legal fees linked to his defense. The city will also be responsible for the remittance of Greg's back pay while he was on suspension leave.

Now that the entire process is over, you must consider how the judge's decision will affect your credibility as well as the conduct and discipline of the Municipal Streets Department employees. You also anticipate a written report from the judge informing you of the reason the department failed to prove its case against Greg. You expect the report will contain a set of instructions that will safeguard against a similar outcome in the future.

Upon reflection, why do you suppose the union took a position in defense of Greg? What suddenly changed the minds of the six employees who had been informally protesting Greg's substandard performance for a protracted period? What do you suppose the court's instructions will be?

Nine

The Perils of Bureaucracy: A *Fait Accompli* in Public Sector Organizations

The rank of Battalion Chief in the 254-member Harrowgate County Fire Department is a prestigious position. Even more impressive is the title that goes along with it: Executive Officer/Operations Division (XO/OD). You had been a captain for the past eight years of your 20 years on the job. During this lengthy period of time, you served in various job descriptions after graduating from the training academy. The assignments are detailed in Table 1.

On the first day of your new duty assignment, you report to the Chief of Department, a matter of protocol for any member assigned to Fire Department Headquarters. Chief Stanley Parker welcomes you to FDHQ, and indicates that your reputation for service excellence has preceded you. He further acknowledges that your career to date has prepared you well for the new position as the XO/OD. You listen attentively to the Chief's brief remarks, keeping in mind he has made it quite clear that your wide-range of operational, investigative, and administrative experience are characteristics that are admired by all members of the department. Coincident with your career resume, your professional credibility is an additional impressive attribute. Needless to say, Chief Parker expects much from you.

Next, you are formally introduced to Deputy Chief Kenneth Nixon, the Chief of the Operations Division. Nixon is the individual who will be your immediate superior officer. You have known DC Nixon for all of the 20 years you have been employed by the department. As a matter of fact, Ken Nixon was in the fire academy training class that graduated as you began your basic firefighter training. In many ways, he helped guide and counsel you during your first few months on the job. Inasmuch as your respective careers diverged considerably from that point forward, you have always been grateful for his encouragement and support when you joined the department.

Table 1.   Assignments

Firefighter	Ladder Company 7	4 Years
Firefighter	Engine Company 44	2 Years
Firefighter	Rescue Company 8	1 Year
Lieutenant	Division of Training	2 Years
Lieutenant	Engine Company 22	2 Years
Lieutenant	Hazardous Materials Company 1	1 Year
Captain	Ladder Company 5	3 Years
Captain	Arson Investigation Bureau	2 Years
Captain	Fire Prevention Bureau	1 Year
Captain	Urban Search & Rescue Squad	2 Years

Most of the above companies are situated in Harrowgate's urban center and, typically, are the busiest fire stations in the county.

Ken Nixon served for two years as a firefighter on an engine company in a suburban area of the county. It is generally acknowledged that he had minimal firefighting experience during this assignment. Thereafter, Nixon was transferred to the department's Community Relations Bureau, where he served for seven years. Except for a six-month assignment as a battalion chief's driver and aide, Nixon served in a number of positions in the Administrative Division for the remainder of his career to date.

Although highly regarded for his administrative skills (Nixon had written many of the department's directives, orders, and procedures), he lacked the firefighting and command and leadership experience a member could attain only by working in a firehouse. Nixon acknowledges and understands these shortcomings, as does everyone who works for the Harrowgate County Fire Department. Rank and file members pejoratively refer to Nixon as "Swivel-chair Kenny."

During the first staff meeting you attend, Chief of Department Stanley Parker assigns DC Nixon the profoundly important task of reviewing firefighter safety practices during emergency operations. DC Nixon, knowing his limitations concerning such an important matter as this, delegates the responsibility to you, which you accept with enthusiasm. As a matter of fact, the issue of firefighter safety has been an ongoing topic of concern to yourself as well as the firefighting forces and the union representing the firefighter's local.

You are quick to commence a review of the subject beginning with a survey questionnaire administered to all members of the department. You believe the feedback will significantly improve the quality of your assessment and succeeding recommendations. Once the survey forms are collected and the information collated, company commanders are instructed to make individual appointments with you to review and discuss the findings. Of course, this method is time-consuming, but you, nevertheless, are certain the content and credibility of your conclusions will be well-served by this process.

DC Nixon requests periodic progress reports, which you deliver once or twice each week. Because he answers directly to the Chief of Department, Nixon wants the process accelerated to ensure its implementation at the earliest possible date and minimize the likelihood that Chief Parker will become impatient with the lack of results.

Although the process is lengthily, you insist it is worthwhile. The people who fight the fires know what is best. The conscientious and painstaking development of the report is, therefore, a sensible and worthwhile investment in time and energy. You ensure DC Nixon that every effort will be made to complete the investigation as rapidly as possible. Perhaps more so than anyone assigned to the executive staff, you know the consequences of insufficient practices in the past. Once implemented, they often fail due to the lack of adequate planning and research.

You think to yourself as you leave DC Nixon's office. The reason the members and employees have so little respect for the headquarters executive staff is the perception that they are out of touch with the real-world of firefighting. You intend to compellingly defend your position on this matter, not only to maintain your own trustworthiness among the rank and file members but the department's credibility as well. Perhaps this will be the start of something new. If the process fails, it will send a signal to the rank and file members that the staff's business-as-usual, out-of-touch approach to problem-solving will be maintained.

After two months of data and information collection, you are prepared to organize and submit a set of recommendations. You judge that the rank and file is satisfied you have studied the matter deliberately. They look forward to the publication of the report and its corresponding orders and procedures. DC Nixon receives the 20-page document with copies for the Chief of Department and the headquarters executive staff, each stamped, "FIRST DRAFT."

At the next staff meeting, you see that your report is not included on the agenda. The meeting proceeds as usual. Afterward, you ask DC Nixon when the document will be discussed among the executive staff. He tells you he has not yet completed his review of it. Nearly one month has passed, and there is no indication the report has been scheduled for review and discussion. Meanwhile, the rank and file members are getting restless. Since they voluntarily contributed to the process, they anxiously await its release, in part to determine how much their input really mattered. Once again, you ask DC Nixon when the report will be submitted to the executive staff for review. To protect yourself against unwarranted criticism from any source, the request for the information is submitted in writing. No answer is received.

In the middle of the third month, you begin to receive telephone calls from company commanders in the Operations Division. They indicate that the rank and file members have become increasingly frustrated over the lack of attention the staff, namely you, are giving to their safety concerns. The appearance of indifference regarding this critical subject is affecting morale among the firefighting forces. It is also influencing the long-term respect and admiration they have historically had for you. You find these circumstances disturbing.

An undercurrent of firehouse chatter implies that you have been a huge disappointment since your transfer to department headquarters; that you actually misled the membership by asking them to participate in the survey. Why? You did your best. You prepared and submitted a thorough report. You did everything you always believed should have been traditionally done in matters of this significance while you were a member of the firefighting force. How did this happen?

At the end of the third month, once more you ask DC Nixon for an update. He offers an ambiguous, indistinct reply. Is the report dying a slow death in Nixon's in-basket? Why hasn't Chief Parker demanded the report? Worse, is someone intentionally trying to undermine your work? While you ponder your next move in this bureaucratic chess game, you receive an anonymous typewritten note. The author advises you that he or she has learned from Stanley Parker's aide that the Chief is furious over the fact that the report has not been presented for his review. Chief Parker has reportedly indicated to certain colleagues his displeasure with you for not completing the report as directed. Parker hinted that his decision to assign you to the department's executive staff may have been a mistake.

What is more, Parker and Nixon are the closest of friends, professionally and socially. If you decide to contact the Chief of Department directly to attend to this matter, you are not only formally violating the chain of command but also risk damaging your relationship with both Parker and Nixon. If you fail to act, Parker's perceptions about you will be validated in his mind.

Meanwhile, nothing is being done to upgrade firefighter safety during emergency operations. You know it. Everyone knows it. If there is a catastrophic incident at a fire scene, everyone will blame you for your seeming indifference. To yourself, you question the motive as to why DC Nixon has failed to advance the report. You wonder why Chief Parker hasn't directly inquired as to the reason the report has not made it to a staff-level conference. Many potential reasons come to mind, including: the bureaucracy; "swivel-chair" executives; the Nixon-Parker friendship; individual and department credibility; anger among the troops, and, above all other considerations, firefighter safety.

You are on probation as a Battalion Chief with five years to retirement. This is your occupational Waterloo. How do you responsibly solve this problem? Is there a way, given the political environment of the organization, that the report can be moved forward? How can you tactfully explain this state of affairs to the company officers?

Ten

The Report is Past-due: Publish or Perish!

Your interview with the Deputy Commissioner went reasonably well. You have applied for a non-classified job description with the state Department of Community Affairs. The job you seek is a position in the department's Special Liaison Office (SLO). The office provides inspectional and support services to local municipal governments throughout the state. Essentially, the job involves monitoring municipal governments to ensure compliance with state regulations relating to their respective practices and procedures. Your past employment history has been exclusively in the private sector where you held positions in quality assurance and efficiency management. If you are fortunate enough to get the job, it will be your first experience working for a government agency.

Nearly one month passes before you receive a congratulatory letter from the Department of Community Affairs. The letter directs you to report to its capitol city facility on a date indicated in the correspondence. In so doing, you receive three days of orientation and training to prepare you for your activities as a member of the department's Special Liaison Office. You also are issued a *SLO Guidebook* that will assist in the municipal government evaluation process.

Altogether, there are five groups consisting of identical staffing levels within the department's Special Liaison Office. Each group of six employees and a group supervisor is assigned a region of the state for monitoring and reviewing purposes. Typically, a group spends about one month in a particular community examining various and sundry municipal documents. After which, the group is responsible for submitting a written report to the commissioner's office for perusal before it is forwarded once more to the governor's office. Upon completion of the training regimen, you are introduced to

31

your group supervisor, Ms. Eileen Crosby. Ms. Crosby enjoys titled status with the state government. She has been a classified employee working for the Department of Community Affairs for 13 years. She supervises a group of six, non-titled employees.

Once a group descends upon a particular jurisdiction, each group member is assigned to review one or more municipal departments. The entire review process in a single jurisdiction takes about two months to complete. Each group member prepares a first draft report while on-site utilizing a lap-top computer assigned to each individual. A comprehensive report of the group's findings, conclusions, and recommendations is prepared thereafter. As a matter of custom and practice, each group member submits a draft document to the group supervisor containing an assessment of the assigned municipal departments. The group supervisor then carefully examines each submitted draft before preparing an all-inclusive report that will be sent to the commissioner.

The draft prepared by the group supervisor is "formatted" by one of the two Special Liaison Office secretaries in order to ensure that headings and subheadings are consistent in all documents that will eventually be sent to the governor. After the draft is formatted, it is reviewed by one of the two attorneys working on the commissioner's legal staff. This legal staff is often overwhelmed with documents to review, as well as with the time-consuming necessity of preparing for testimony in court appearances on behalf of the Department of Community Affairs and preparing materials for the legislative process. As deemed appropriate, the legal team may prepare an addendum to be added to the report.

A final step in the process requires that each municipality that is reviewed by the Special Liaison Office group receives a copy of the report once it is checked thoroughly by the governor's office staff and approved for dissemination. These reports delineate the measures that must be undertaken by the municipality to come into compliance with state mandates, and to provide the opportunity for correction prior to the next Department of Community Affairs inspection. There have been instances where the report has been challenged by the municipality, which requires additional review and response time. Every effort is made to provide an administrative review process when such a challenge occurs.

To simplify, the steps in each Special Liaison Office municipal government review are as follows:

1. The SPO group arrives at a particular municipality, and each group member receives an assignment;
2. The SPO group examines municipal departments, and associated documents;

3. After a review of their respective department(s), a first draft report is prepared on lap-top computers while on-site by individual group members;
4. First draft copies received from each member are reviewed by the group supervisor, and a comprehensive draft report is subsequently prepared;
5. The comprehensive draft report prepared by the group supervisor is formatted by an office secretary;
6. The draft is forwarded to the commissioner's office for review by the commissioner and the legal staff. An addendum is added if necessary;
7. The report (in its final draft format) is forwarded to the governor's office for review; and
8. Once approved by the governor, the document is sent to the municipal government's chief executive for study and compliance.

After eight months of service with the department, your previous employment experience begins to shape your every thought. You know that the process is slow and could be made more efficient and effective. You have heard a number of criticisms and concerns expressed by co-workers in the Special Liaison Office, as well as by fellow group members, and municipal government agency employees. These observations are summarized as follows:

Due to the length of time it takes the Special Liaison Office group to conduct a review of their respective departments, municipal employees consider it a necessary but intrusive imposition that interferes with the performance of their respective duties and responsibilities;

Because each group member must submit a rough draft to the group's supervisor for editing and re-writing, the process is more costly and takes longer than necessary to complete;

Formatting by an office secretary takes time, since there are so many reports to be organized;

The commissioner's legal staff is overworked, and protracted delays often result at this juncture in the process;

The governor's office expects the frequency of Special Liaison Office reports to increase in time and number in the next fiscal year;

The non-supervisory workforce of the Special Liaison Office are not classified employees; and

If the Special Liaison Group fails to fulfill its legal mandate in a timely manner, it is unlikely that it will be allowed to conduct its work as presently constituted.

The commissioner is feeling the pressure to reduce production time and, concomitantly, enhance the quality of the reports. There is some speculation and rumor that the Department of Community Affairs will face a reduction in its budget allocation for the next fiscal year if there is not a substantial improvement in the Special Liaison Office component of the agency. The commissioner learns of your background and technical expertise as a private sector employee. You are summoned to his office. Although he acknowledges that you have relatively limited experience in the public sector, he asks you to recommend ways and means to improve the department's service delivery. He implies that your judgments and opinions will be critical to continuance of the Special Liaison Office and the retention of its non-titled employees.

After agreeing to the request and leaving the commissioner's office, you realize that no mention was made as to whether or not Ms.Crosby had been advised of his decision. You further understand that you hold the future of 30 or more individuals in your hands. You begin to think. Maybe the system is slow because it was designed to be unhurried. How can government protocols be streamlined if they are intended to be slow? Will accelerating the process increase the number of reports, but neglect critical issues? Isn't quality more important than quantity, even in the public sector?

All things considered, you must do something; *status quo* is not acceptable. Everything is on the proverbial table for analysis. What measures will you recommend to improve the process? Remember, for every criticism there must be a recommended solution.

Eleven

Midnight in the Central District: The Big Red Truck That Went Away

Stapleton is an eight square mile city with a diverse population of 67,144. About 60% of its residential and commercial structures are considered "new construction" (post 1980s) that mandates the installation of fire detection and suppression systems in accordance with city codes. There are no industrial facilities in the city.

The city fire department was once an exclusively volunteer service staffed by unpaid professionals. The rapid growth of the city during the past fifteen years (the population increased from approximately 28,000 to 67,000-plus) made it obvious that maintaining a volunteer fire department was becoming less and less feasible. Nine years ago, four paid professional firefighters, one assigned to each of the city's four fire stations, were hired to work from 8:00 A.M. until 4:00 P.M. when the availability of volunteer responders began to diminish appreciably during daytime hours.

Over the next two years, volunteerism nationwide began to decline significantly. Stapleton experienced this phenomenon as well. Furthermore, these circumstances heightened risk exposure, which caused fire insurance rates to escalate for small business owners. This consequence made it almost cost-prohibitive to begin or retain commercial enterprises in the city. These conditions literally forced the city to migrate rapidly to a fully paid fire department.

Two parcels of land were acquired, one on each side of town, on which two multi-company, "super stations" were constructed to house the reorganized fire department's east district and west district operations. Coverage area for each "super station" was approximately four square miles. Three of the four old volunteer firehouses were soon closed and demolished to make way for much needed community playgrounds. Public reaction to both the fire department's facility relocations and the creation of three new neighborhood playgrounds was overwhelmingly favorable.

Only one of the old volunteer firehouses remains open. The station houses a single engine company staffed by full-time firefighters. It is situated in a one-half square mile tract in the central district of the city, the population of which largely consists of minority-owned residential and business properties. Most of the structures in the central district pre-date 1940 construction standards, making them susceptible to rapid fire acceleration.

The city administration has ordered this last remaining single-company station to be closed by the end of the current year. The city wants to sell the building and the fire equipment to avoid ongoing and increasing maintenance costs. The city plans to use the money from the sales to purchase upgrades for the police and fire department computerized telecommunications center at city hall. Without the sale of the building, the necessary upgrades will have to be set aside for future consideration. The fire chief agrees with the decision. It is now October 2nd.

When the neighborhood residents, business owners, and clergy learn of this decision, they immediately serve notice of their objection to the proposal to the mayor and city council. An organized protest commences in the form of an informational picket line posted at their neighborhood firehouse that is designated for closure. Demonstrations begins at an early morning hour and continue uninterrupted until late in the evening each day.

The city sent representatives to meet with civic, business, and religious leaders to explain the rationale for their decision to close the firehouse. Public officials contend that an exhaustive study by an independent consultant concluded that the closing would not jeopardize public safety. As a matter of fact, the nearest area "super station" is only seven blocks from the intersection of their neighborhood firehouse. According to the consultant's assessment, the nearby "super station" affords the community the necessary and appropriate protection according to national and regional fire protection standards.

Nevertheless, protests continue. Residents counter that the firehouse has historically been the center of community activity. What is more, the firehouse has sentimental value; many of their family members had been volunteer firefighters for three generations. Children know the firehouse is a safe place if they need help. One group has even started investigating how to obtain historical building status as a way to maintain the building. This group feels that having the building will provide a rationale for maintaining an active force.

Elected officials are becoming more and more uneasy about the obvious political fallout over the decision to close the firehouse. They estimate that over 96% of central district residents and business owners oppose the decision to close the firehouse. The mayor and members of council will also find it difficult to justify keeping the building open in the central district since other neighborhood stations were closed throughout the city to make way for the construction of the two "super stations." Consultant fees in the amount of $24,000 for the evaluation of the city's public safety needs will also have to be explained to the balance of city taxpayers not directly affected by the decision to shut down the firehouse.

Still, residents protest. No matter the justification, they believe the third-year mayor and some members of the city council are insensitive to community issues and concerns. Some even suggest it is because most non-white businesses and homes are located in the central district. It is mid-December. The firehouse remains open and the picketing continues. As the mayor's Public Information Officer, you begin to think of the alternatives you may one day soon discuss with him. After all, next year, he will be up for reelection along with three of the five members of city council.

During the overnight hours of December 23rd, the central district engine company is dispatched to a report of a fire in a contiguous neighborhood. The response turns out to be a false alarm. While the engine company is out of quarters, the city Public Works Department padlocks the firehouse doors on orders from the mayor. Public Works Department employees place a large, thin-gauged metal sign on the overhead door of the station that reads, "FIREHOUSE CLOSED: NEAREST FIREHOUSE AT WEST END AVENUE & 3RD STREET." Over the fire department radio, the engine company is instructed to relocate its apparatus to the city's Maintenance Shops, and thereafter, the vehicle is placed in out-of-service status. Company members are transported in police department vehicles back to the central district fire station in order to retrieve their personal belongings. Firefighters from the now-closed central district firehouse will be reassigned to the two "super stations."

When the neighborhood residents awake in the morning, they hear a rumor that the firehouse has been vacated. When the pickets assemble, the allegation is substantiated. They immediately and forcibly accuse the city administration of cowardly closing the firehouse in the darkness of night, acting against the will of the people. They vow to bring civil suit against the city, as well as petition the grand jury to investigate the transmission of a false alarm of fire, a violation of the state's criminal code. They demand the city explain why the firehouse was surreptitiously evacuated in the middle of the night. Things are beginning to unravel quickly for the mayor. It's time for some serious political damage control.

The mayor attends a protest rally in the neighborhood. He apologizes for the way the matter was handled, and criticizes the fire chief for the decision. With the reelection campaign just months away, he knows he will not receive support from the antagonized voters of the central district. He needs a plurality of their votes to remain in office. After the protest, the mayor asks you for advice on how to stop the bleeding. He insists the decision to close the fire-house was the correct choice. However, it has placed him on the horns of a dilemma. How can he convince his constituents in the central district that it was a correct decision? Is there an alternative no one in city hall has considered that would appease the community, without being an affront to the rest of the city's taxpayers? How will the mayor, council, and fire chief recover from this public relations nightmare?

Twelve

Mercy!: Floor-by-floor, the Nurses Silently Roar

Mercy County Medical Center (MCMC) is public facility located in a rural section of the county. It is a very quiet place: there is no traffic or crowd noise; there are no aircraft over flights; and there are no children at play anywhere near the hospital building. Ambulances have no reason to use their audible warning devices when approaching the hospital's emergency room portico. In sum, the setting is quite pastoral. By reputation, it is a first-rate place to work.

There are no other public medical centers in the county, and the nearest private hospital is located 20 miles away in Lawson City. It is an old facility with modern equipment. However, the atmosphere at the city's Birch-Lawson Hospital is unlike that of MCMC. There is a good deal of traffic congestion in the vicinity of the hospital and plenty of noise to go along with it. Yet, there is very little turnover of hospital employees. Birch-Lawson Hospital is a union shop. A majority of its professional and non-professional workforce live within the city limits.

Although the MCMC physical plant is nearly 70 years old, it is well-maintained, neat, and clean. It too is equipped with state of the art technology for diagnostics and patient care. The workforce is non-union. A majority of professional and non-professional employees live in residential subdivisions within a seven mile radius of the hospital. The center's nursing staff is composed of 30 Registered Nurses. By schedule, 21 RNs are on-duty during the 24-hour period. Other than annual cost of living increases (based on regional COLA data), pay raises and promotional considerations are based on formal education, length of service, and continuing education training program attendance. From time to time, nurses are sent to continuing education courses by hospital administrators. More often, nurses attend these courses on their own time and at their own expense.

39

The RNs daily routine is consistent, routine, uniform, and predictable. Work shifts and floor assignments are rotated. Staffing levels are based on a proportionate need basis on three, eight-hour shifts. These working arrangements have remained constant for over 20 years. There has been no indication that the nursing staff is unsatisfied with these working conditions.

Nursing staff performance, although not exceptional, has been generally satisfactory. However, morale has never been particularly very good. Sick leave is relatively high among the RNs, and duty shifts are frequently understaffed. Squabbling between the RNs, and between the RNs and non-medical employees is a daily occurrence. Physicians complain to administrators from time to time about their belligerence as well. Perhaps worst of all, patients have complained on occasion that the nurses are discourteous, indifferent, and unresponsive to their needs. All of these are indicators of low morale on the part of the RNs.

Since most of the behavioral infractions have been considered relatively minor, hospital administrators have had a tendency to ignore the matter. At one point they were convinced that these antagonisms were the cumulative effect of the stresses that nurses experience on the job. However, periodic mandatory stress counseling sessions failed to alleviate the antipathy. Hospital executives firmly believe that if morale was really all that bad, at least one or more of the nurses would have resigned by now. Hospital executives would then be able to ascertain the scope of the problem during the conduct of exit interviews. This hasn't happened. As a matter of fact, during a recent state-wide meeting of public hospital administrators, the group learns three things of interest: 1) the regional economy is in decline; 2) the unemployment rate is approaching six percent; and (3) there are more RNs in the region than there are available nursing positions in both public and private hospitals.

During the lunch break, MCMC executives ponder the issue of low morale among the nursing staff. They clearly understand that any nurse who resigns from the facility will have difficulty finding employment elsewhere. If a nurse decided to work at a private physician's office, he or she would lose the health care benefits as well as the guaranteed annual salary increase currently provided by MCMC. Furthermore, there are limited opportunities for the leveraging of a nursing career to a non-medical job description.

If MCMC is such a high-quality place to work and employment opportunities, particularly within the nursing profession, are severely limited, why do the nurses appear so unhappy? What do they want? How will we learn the answers to these questions? If and when we do discover the answers, how will we resolve the issues?

You have observed the RN's conduct throughout your two years of employment with MCMC as an assistant to the Deputy Administrator. Hospital executives look to you for help. They do not want any of their biases or personal relationships to interfere in the search for the answer to the mystery. How will you begin your detective work?

Thirteen

Sweeping the Budget Crisis under the Rug: Blaming the Little Guys for a Big Problem

It's that time of the year again. It's the occasion for your annual investment in mass quantities of aspirin tablets (extra strength!). Yes, it's those dreaded two words that cause muscle tension, stomach aches, and sleepless nights: Budget Preparation. Although the process is troublesome and irritating at times, it cannot be avoided. Worse yet, there are no secret hideouts in town hall for you to hunker down for the next two months. Vacation leave is not an alternative either. What's a person to do?

By state law, the Town of Donovan, a one-half square mile village with a population 1,683, must begin the groundwork on an initial draft of the municipal budget for the next fiscal year. You have been involved in this process for three years as Donovan's Chief Financial Officer. Prior to becoming CFO, you interned in the town's comptroller's office while a public finance student at nearby Vincent James College.

The budget process is clearly a prescriptive procedure. A department head meeting typically kicks off the budget process each year. It is here that the town's elected officials elaborate their policies for the coming year. This year is not unlike the previous three years, with one exception, that is. It is at this annual pre-budget conference that you learn of a significant shortfall in anticipated revenues for the next fiscal period: the state has reduced funding to local communities by 10%.

The mayor and the three-member town council (both non-salaried positions) have directed the department heads to submit their respective budget requests to the CFO with this consequence in mind. You do the math in your head as you stare at the clock on the conference room wall. You are certain service delivery will be adversely affected by a cumulative budget reduction of 10%. You envision an outpouring of citizen complaints throughout the next year as a result.

Once the mayor and council members leave the room, the remaining full-time attendees (yourself [CFO], the Purchasing Agent, Municipal Clerk, Director of the Department of Public Works, Tax Collector) look at one another in bewilderment. If you could read their minds, it would be quite clear to you that the cutbacks are going to cause each one of them a great deal of difficulty in performing their duties in compliance with legal mandates and in harmony with public expectations. They know that you will have the final word on each of their budget requests.

You mentally review the positive and negative concerns for the municipality. Public safety is provided by the State Police at no cost to the Town of Donovan, along with a volunteer fire company and volunteer ambulance squad, also at no cost to the town. Water and sewer utilities and trash removal are the responsibility of the individual homeowner. There are few commercial ratables, and residential subdivisions are built-out. The mean position value (salary and benefits) for the five full-time department heads is $31,000. Salaries range from $2,000 to $5,000 for five part-time employees, the greatest expense is remuneration for the municipal court judge. Part-time employees receive no medical/health care benefits.

As soon as you return to your office, you peruse last year's fiscal budget. In so doing, one seemingly minor line item captures your attention. The aggregate cost of "Janitorial Services" budgeted for the previous year was $53,000, as itemized in Table 2.

Your first thought is to have the town's Purchasing Agent secure price quotes from a private janitorial service company. If a private vendor can provide janitorial services for town hall, why not consider this option as a budget-reducing strategy for next year? You decide to pursue this alternative, and ask the Purchasing Agent to do so in the strictest of confidence. You do not want to upset the two in-house janitors who have been loyal and faithful employees since the new town hall was constructed ten years ago. Furthermore, you want to ensure that each department head remains focused on reducing their budget requests.

Two days later, you and the Purchasing Agent meet in your office. She advises you that there are three private janitorial service companies within a fif-

Table 2.   Last Year's Fiscal Budget

Salaries (Two Employees)	$40,000
Employee Health Care and Medical Benefits	$ 6,000
Employee Uniform Maintenance and Clothing Allowance	$ 2,000
Janitorial Supplies	$ 5,000

"Janitorial Supplies" include, but are not limited to, the following items: Brooms, mops, cleaning fluids, furniture and floor polish, vacuum cleaner bags, cleansers, soaps, etc.

teen mile radius who are interested in providing clean-up services to the Town of Donovan. All three provide similar services to several towns within the indicated geographic area. Their price quotes are competitive, the lowest of the three being $22,800 annually. She cautions you that the service to be provided is very basic: once each day, there is a general clean-up (i.e., tiled floors swept, carpeted floors vacuumed, public restrooms cleaned and re-supplied with paper and soap products, and wastebaskets emptied). Nothing else is included.

During the discussion with the Purchasing Agent, your secretary apologetically interrupts the meeting. She needs several packages of paper for the office copy machine. One of the janitors retrieves the necessary items from the supply closet in your office and carries them to the countertop alongside the copy machine near the secretary's desk. Fortunately, he did not overhear any of the conversation between yourself and the Purchasing Agent.

Alone once more, you find that there are two employees assigned to the Department of Public Works who will retire in the forthcoming fiscal year. Good fortune! These positions can be filled by the town hall janitors, obviating the concern for their possible unemployment. It seems like a no-brainer. The town will save $30,200, almost 10% of the budget for next year. Department heads may not have to drastically trim their budgets after all. Their worries about the impact of budget reductions on their respective duties and responsibilities, service delivery obligations, and related public expectations will be short-lived.

You are convinced that privatizing Janitorial Services is the solution to this year's annual budget predicament. While walking down the hall to meet with the mayor, you become suddenly awash in an odd sensation about the recommendation you are about to make. You step outside to reflect on this strange feeling before going any further. It is a beautiful day. One of the janitors is watering the flowers; the other is sweeping the walkway and curbside alongside the building. They are there, but you don't really see them. You are preoccupied with your reservations about the decision.

You ask yourself these questions: Am I acting in haste? Have I given this matter the attention and careful thought it deserves? Have I overlooked something that might have changed my mind? Are there better strategies to address these issues? A voice whispers in your ear. . . "Better postpone the meeting and give this issue a little more thought."

Fourteen

Saturday Night Live: A Walk in the Park

The sparsely populated town of Ewing's Point is a tranquil, suburban community known for its skyline of trees. The lifestyle of its residents is likened to that of a typical small New England town. People know their neighbors; they care about one another. They even know the first names of the town's eight-member police force. Many of the townspeople are (or have been) members of the volunteer fire company and ambulance squad.

Every Saturday (weather permitting) during the Spring, Summer, and Fall months, the town's Parks and Playgrounds Department sponsors free outdoor evening concerts in Pine Tree Park that begin at 7:00 P.M. The entertainment is provided by the region's high school music departments and music schools in the tri-state area. A military band from one of the four services usually performs at least one annual recital as well. From time to time, amateur comedians present stand-up routines and vaudeville acts. All in all, the activities make for enjoyable evenings in the park. Although residents as well as non-residents are welcomed to attend the activities in the park, the majority of attendees from the area are senior citizens. The park concerts are a part of the town's history and have been a staple of community tradition and pride in Ewing's Point for over a century.

As previously indicated, there is no admission fee. That said, the entertainment provided is not without cost to the town. Of course, the expenses associated with the productions are paid for by the resident taxpayers. The costs include overtime pay for two employees of the Parks and Playgrounds Department (setting up and taking down folding lawn chairs, and post-event clean-up work), and overtime pay for two police officers who provide park security.

During the off-season, the International Brotherhood of Electrical Workers formally notified town officials that a union electrician from the Ewing's Point Maintenance Department must be on location at Pine Tree Park if the facility is to be illuminated for any special event after sundown. This stipulation also necessitates payment at the overtime rate for the assigned maintenance worker. Likewise, utility expenses increase when this circumstance occurs.

As town manager, you know it will be necessary to either recommend a tax increase or a fee for attendees to the mayor and council in view of these escalating costs if these events are to continue. Since the concerts are the town's signature activity, you know that eliminating the park concerts (or even scaling back their frequency) is absolutely out of the question. It is as certain a political death as touching a subway's third rail. You understand that senior citizens on fixed incomes may not be able to afford any tax increase or a fee for attendance, and know they are a potent political force in the town. You also know that things cannot remain *status quo*.

What are the options? What will you propose to the mayor and council at the next budget meeting? Your recommendations must be rank-ordered descending from "First Best Option."

Fifteen

Third-to-First: One Out

The Port Harrison Police Department is a civil service organization consisting of seventy-five sworn members, fifteen of whom are eligible for promotion to the rank of sergeant. However, at the present time only three positions need to be filled. The department has announced that a written examination has been scheduled for November, six months from the present day. It is a time of great anticipation and anxiety; not only for the eligible candidates but for all of the members and employees of the department. Retirements and promotions mean that changes in personnel are forthcoming. Most are concerned with what is likely to occur, which include the following: Who will be promoted?; What type of boss will he or she be?; Will there be transfers?; How will these promotions influence the future of the organization?; and How will the 12 members who are not elevated in rank act in response?

Some of the more interesting conversation and speculation revolves around two individuals who are eligible to take the examination. John Counts and Steve Crawford joined the department eleven years ago. They attended the police training academy together and have remained friends ever since. There has been some healthy competition between the two for years as each worked hard to collect "excellent" ratings on their respective annual evaluations. Arrest and performance records exceed those of their peers. Both have received numerous official department commendations. Both men possess exceptional credentials for the position of sergeant.

As Patrol Division Commander, you value their service to the department and the community. You are confident that two of the three promotions will be John Counts and Steve Crawford, and look forward to having them on your staff as patrol supervisors. As days turn into weeks, John and Steve industriously study for the written test. They agree to continue their pleasant rivalry by not studying together. To them, the real test is which one would finish ahead of the other; not which one will be promoted.

Both John Counts and Steve Crawford have impressive resumes to go along with their distinguished service record with the Port Harrison Police Department. John Counts graduated from the state college *Magna Cum Laude* and recently completed a six year military obligation with the Air Force Reserve. John fulfilled his service requirement by serving six months of active duty followed by five years and six months of reserve duty status, during which he attended weekend drills once each month for the balance of his service time. He entered the USAFR as a second lieutenant and was discharged honorably with the rank of major. His military service record was a good indicator of future performance: he always exceeded standards and maintained an unblemished record throughout his military service.

Likewise, Steve Crawford served in the military. Steve did not attend college. Instead, he enlisted in the Marines and served four years of full-time active service, one year of which was served overseas. He too had an excellent military service record. In fact, he won a Silver Star during combat on foreign soil. John frequently teases Steve by referring to him affectionately as "Enlisted Man." Steve counters by calling John, "General Counts" when the verbal sparring begins.

For John Counts the forthcoming promotional written exam will represent a particular challenge; he is not a good test taker. He always excelled during the interview portion of the promotional examination process in the Air Force. The same was true during the police entrance exam protocol; passable on the written, excellent on the oral board portion. It was the latter assessment that always put him over the top.

Conversely, Steve Crawford always did very well on the written portion of any examination. Steve always knew the subject very well, but often failed to articulate his responses effectively during the oral board portion of an exam. The former quality was enough to put him over the top.

Weeks turned into months, and October became November. It was the time for the candidates to take the written test for advancement to sergeant. John and Steve wished one another the best of luck and took their places among the department's candidates for promotion. Three agonizing months later, the list was posted. Those that scored high enough on the written test would be invited to participate in the oral board examination. The posted listing surprised most and shocked a few. Steve Crawford finished in first place on the written exam; John Counts finished fourth. Although he heartily congratulated his friend, John was humiliated at not having scored high enough to qualify for the oral board exam.

As a matter of practice, the Police Chief and the executive staff met with each of the fifteen candidates individually after the written exam list was posted. Each received formal notice of his or her score followed by a brief discussion of the candidate's respective strengths and weaknesses. When John Counts entered the room, there was a noticeable aura of apprehension and uneasiness among those in attendance. The look of disappointment seemed to be permanently affixed to John's face. It was surrealistic. He seemed to be in another dimension not of this world. The Police Chief opened the discussion with the customary expression of gratitude for John's performance excellence throughout his career with the department. John's face remained transfixed. It was difficult for the chief to get to the point of the subject. He knew how difficult it would be for John to learn of the reason for his fourth-place finish. John had missed finishing third by mere percentage points. John also learned that Steve had been awarded points for his full-time military veteran status that were enough to move his final ranking from third place to first on the list.

Naturally, everyone, including Steve, tried to cheer-up John, but on the day of the promotion ceremony, John was seething. To him, he had been wronged. How could Steve be awarded military veteran status points simply because he was in the full-time service? Hadn't he been an officer in the Air Force? Didn't he spend six years of his life in the service of his country, albeit in the reserves? Didn't he receive a Bachelor of Arts degree with high honors? Something was out of balance.

Nevertheless, John's performance remains well above department standards even after the letdown. He never had a bad word to say about Steve. They remain good friends. Even though John's new patrol supervisor is one of the newly promoted sergeants, he seems unusually ambivalent about this personnel decision. If anything, John is angry at "The System" that caused him to be eliminated from the promotional process, rather than a particular individual. John did become oddly militaristic immediately after the three promotions were officially announced, however. He seemed to be acting out of character emotionally. Unlike his previous behavior, he rarely stopped to talk with colleagues. He appeared strange and distant. By May, it is more apparent than ever that John needs professional help to cope with his distress. Although his job performance remains constant, his social relationships on and off-duty continue to deteriorate. You begin to hear innuendos of John's rage whenever the topic of promotions is brought up in conversation. You worry that the perceived cause of John's frustration ("The System") is actually the department itself, and its executive staff. If these intimations are accurate, you wonder how John's persistent anger will eventually manifest itself.

Lately, you learn by way of an anonymous letter that John Counts laughingly remarked that he would have the final say with regard to the issue of department promotions. The correspondence infers that he had his hand on his holstered service weapon when he made the comment. The letter further insinuates that the men and women of the Patrol Division are becoming increasingly concerned with John's "bizarre" behavior. This is one unsigned note that cannot be unceremoniously dispatched to the wastepaper basket. You metaphorically observe ominous clouds in the distance. A cloudburst could come at any minute. How will you shelter yourself and everyone else from what appears to be an approaching storm? You hope this phenomenon will pass; the sooner the better.

You are reasonably certain that John will object to the proposition of a psychiatric evaluation, voluntary or forced. You don't want to make an already bad situation any worse by stigmatizing John among his coworkers, which will likely further aggravate him. However, you cannot deny that John's worsening condition requires professional attention for his (and the department's) long-term well-being.

As Patrol Division Commander, you know that the duty and responsibility of referring him to a department psychologist for appraisal and treatment initially resides with you. First, department policy requires that you prepare a written report that assesses John's present behavior and present behavioral consequences, and, if left untreated, his likely future behavior and resultant consequences for presentation to the Chief of Police. The chief must approve any recommendation you make with regard to this matter.

What observations and conclusions will your four-columned assessment report to the Chief of Police include?

Sixteen

Propose or Oppose:
What's an "Advocate" to Do?

The evening's festivities could not be more exciting. It is election night, and Janet Gleeson has been chosen to be the state's first female governor. You are at her campaign headquarters to attend the celebration. Your presence is not a happenstance. You and the governor-elect have known one another since college when the two of you were sorority sisters. Since that time, you have followed her ascension from Assembly Woman to her forthcoming inauguration as governor. Not only have you been an enthusiastic admirer, but a contributor as well, both financially and through generous, voluntary legal counsel over the years.

As Janet Gleeson was preparing to run for a seat on the State Assembly, she called asking you to join her campaign staff as an unsalaried, part-time worker. The full-time staff needed someone who had the candidate's confidence, respect, loyalty, and trust. You were asked to review the various and sundry issues likely to surface during the campaign and prepare a series of position papers based on legal research and your own informed opinion.

Janet Gleeson credits her election to the Assembly in large measure to your untiring work on her campaign staff. Her gracious and flattering remarks during the election night party 14 years ago still resonate with you. You were present once more throughout her successful campaign for the State Senate. Tonight, you are with her once again.

During a private conversation, Gleeson asks that you consider a position on her staff. She intends to create an Office of Public Advocate by executive order upon assuming office, and would like to appoint you its Executive Director. Establishment of the office had been a plank in her platform when she was received the nomination of her party as its candidate for governor. Joining the governor's executive staff will necessitate the temporary suspension of your successful and lucrative law practice for the duration of your public service. The decision is not the least bit difficult. Since you and the governor-elect passionately share the same values and political philosophy, you accept the challenge that the new office will demand.

During the intervening months between the election and inauguration, the governor's transition team prepared a number of policy papers for each executive branch staff officer and department head appointed to serve in the new administration. As you carefully peruse the manuscript, you notice a provision that directs the public advocate's office to submit proposals on substantive public policy matters to the governor's political adviser prior to undertaking further action. The requirement does not seem unreasonable.

Once the real work begins, it is clear that most issues (i.e., questions, complaints, and referrals) processed by your office can be easily and effectively handled by your staff.

Months pass before a matter crosses your desk that requires immediate personal attention.

The Association of Certified State Paralegals is petitioning the Office of Public Advocate for support in co-sponsoring legislation that will obviate the need for Attorney's-at-Law in the preparation of certain legal documents, such as wills, minor real estate transactions, and small business corporation papers. The paralegals intend to argue that their services are more convenient and more expedient than a typical law office is able to provide, and significantly less expensive as well. They will assert that the public interest will be better served by their involvement in these minor legal procedures. The state's Small Business Association and the Chamber of Commerce support any change in the law that will lessen the burden on small business entrepreneurs. The Attorney's Guild, of which you are a member, opposes any piece of legislation that will extend the power and authority of paralegals. They insist serious mistakes will be made that will cause harm to clients and, therefore, be contrary to the public interest in the final analysis.

You are inclined to support the proposition and forward the proposal along with your recommendation to the governor's political adviser. Shortly thereafter, you learn that the Attorney's Guild contributed a considerable amount of money to Governor Gleeson's political campaigns over the years. In practical terms, the proposed legislation is a good idea; in political terms, it is not. At first, you are relieved to find out that the governor's political adviser intends to ask Gleeson to oppose the legislation. Since you intend to eventually return to private practice, you have no desire to be skewered by your peers in the legal profession.

Upon reflection, however, you realize that failure to support the proposed changes in the law represents an abdication of the public advocate's responsibilities. You also understand that it is only a matter of time before the issue of campaign contributions becomes a matter of public information. When it does, your personal veracity and the integrity of the Office of Public Advocate will be questioned. Being skewered by your peers in the legal profession might not be so bad after all.

You consider the following options:

1. Continue to advocate for the change in the law, and approach the governor directly for her support;
2. Tell the governor that the credibility of the Office of Public Advocate will be jeopardized (and, by extension her own trustworthiness) if she opposes the legislation;
3. Oppose the legislation on the grounds that it will not be a feasible solution to the problem of costly legal fees;
4. Ask the governor to forward the proposed change to her legislative aide for review and later submission to the Assembly for consideration; and/or
5. Resign your position as Executive Director of the Office of Public Advocate and return to your private law practice.

Are there other alternatives that you failed to list? What option(s) will you choose? Why? Are there other issues of concern that you have not considered?

Seventeen

Shame, Shame, Shame: Looking for a Person to Blame

You have been working at a private university's Office of Strategic Planning for six years. The people with whom you work are dedicated professionals; the physical plant is less than 20 years old and well maintained, and; it is 22 miles from the driveway of your house to the green fields of the campus. Although you enjoy the job and the work is interesting and challenging, you have been reading the Sunday newspaper's *Career Prospective* section for the past three months and *the Chronicle for Higher Education*, nevertheless. Opportunities for growth, development, and higher pay are somewhat restricted for those who work for private academic institutions in the region. Moreover, the prospect of advancement at your present workplace in the near future is not promising. In the private sector, there are no job titles with corresponding pay scales.

You are confidant that your experience can be leveraged for a higher paying position with a public college or university. You begin to formulate a personal strategic plan to prepare for employment elsewhere. The timing of the venture is uncanny. Just as you begin to get serious about changing jobs, a professional colleague advises that a non-teaching position for which you are uniquely qualified is open at the Richardson Blame State College. The job description is not unlike that of your current occupation. Taking into account your experience, the salary offer you are likely to receive should be commensurate with your current pay.

The upside to the position is that the state college system operates on job title and pay grade classifications, which is exactly what you want. Upon appointment, you will receive union representation and protection, along with the benefit of job security. In the long term, you will make more money. Richardson Blame State College is in Fitzgerald City approximately 40 miles from your home. There is, however, a caveat to consider that your colleague wants you to know before making the decision to change jobs: The RBSC Administration Office has an embarrassing state-wide reputation for being in a condition of perpetual of disorder. It is at this interval you learn that the college is looking to hire someone who will be able to quickly transform chaos into order in the office. If you apply for and accept the position, the person designated for the task will be you.

After considering the matter for a few days, you notify RBSC Personnel Office that you are interested in the vacant position. Soon thereafter, you present yourself along with your resume to the school's personnel director. The interview that follows is unusually brief, and you are offered the job on the spot. The salary offer is better than you anticipated. Three weeks later, you report to work at the college Administration Office. The orientation meeting with the school's chief administrator goes very well. During the appointment, he advises you that the overriding issue at RBSC is the office's poor standing among the students and faculty. The five clerical employees assigned to the office have the same job title, receive comparable salaries, and are all political appointees. At the conclusion of the meeting, he details the specific repetitive issues that are causing the problems that you will be directed to resolve. They include the following:

- More often than not, specific course materials for students are not ordered, nor are they received, in time for the start of classes;
- Students are often billed two and three times for a particular course;
- Some clerical staff employees frequently arrive late, take more than one hour for their lunch break, and leave early;
- Morale among the clerical staff employees is poor;
- Recurrent absenteeism results in important tasks not getting done;
- There have been occasions (albeit infrequently) when a faculty member fails to receive the course materials that are necessary to prepare for a course of study in a timely manner;
- Habitually, course textbooks are not ordered (or not ordered in sufficient quantity) for the students who must purchase them at the college bookstore;
- Classrooms are assigned to more than one professor at the same time;
- Students who live on campus and do not own cars regularly receive notice of delinquent payment for on-campus parking violations, making them ineligible to register for courses; and
- It is all but impossible to discipline a clerical staff employee.

You request to examine the administration's policy directives along with the rules and regulations, and learn that there are none. You are told that the union representing the clerical staff insists that each and every job-related matter be subject to negotiation. What is more, you get a sense that the administrator is intimidated, not only by the union, but by the political implications as well.

The administrator asks that you begin the review of the staff's practices and procedures at once, and present an action plan to him within a three week period. What measures will you take to assess the staff's functions? What steps will you recommend to overcome the indicated weaknesses and personnel discrepancies in the operation of the Administration Office?

Eighteen

Disaster Planning: The Decision Making Process in Ridgevale

Parkhurst is a seven square mile suburban community (population 16,765) in Stacey County consisting of several "new construction" residential subdivisions and two strip store shopping centers. Neighboring contiguous municipalities are similar in character, population, and geographic area. The largest city, Ridgevale, is approximately 30 miles north of Parkhurst.

Working for the Town of Parkhurst has been intrinsically rewarding. Twelve years ago, you joined the town's volunteer fire company and had the good fortune to work with its many dedicated, unpaid professional men and women. Your membership in the fire company launched your career as Parkhurst's first full-time Director of the Office of Emergency Management (OEM), a position you have held for five years. Being the OEM director in a small town has its share of challenges. Because the fire company and ambulance squad are volunteer services, the mandated personnel training programs can be difficult to facilitate. This condition is not due to the lack of cooperation and support; finding the required time has always been problematical. Scheduling mutual aid training exercises is complicated for the same reason.

The police department's authorized strength has been static for three years since the town has been built-out. There are 27 sworn members and four civilian employees. Training the police force in OEM protocols has been relatively uncomplicated when compared to the volunteer services. There has never been anything less than full cooperation and support from the town's emergency services.

While attending a meeting of municipal, county, and state OEM directors, you are approached by Joe Koacher, Stacey County OEM chief. A deputy director's position is opening in the City of Ridgevale, and he would like you to interview for the job. The decision to pursue and apply for the position in

Ridgevale must be made within a week. Your reputation in the county along with the recommendation of Director Koacher virtually assures you the job if you want it. You know very little about Ridgevale, having been in the city only a few times to attend minor league hockey games at the Pickett Square Arena. There is much to learn, particularly if you are considering a post with the city's OEM staff. Soon you learn the differences between Parkhurst and Ridgevale. As you do, you begin appreciate the challenges ahead.

Ridgevale is a small city with a population of 73,350. Its 13 square mile landmass is comprised of "old construction" residential, commercial, and light industrial zones. It lies in a valley between two mountain ranges, and the terrain is hilly with narrow, steep streets criss-crossing its eastern and western sections. Its largest manufacturing facility (ClearCo) produces industrial strength cleaning fluids. The liquid is "bottled" in plastic containers and stored on the premises until removed by truck or railroad car. A railroad spur is adjacent to the ClearCo™ plant. Once the cargo is removed from the factory, it passes through the city's industrial park area and onto the interstate highway or the parallel CSX Railroad right-of-way. The plant is vital to the city's economic welfare.

There is a man-made lake holding approximately 14 million gallons of water on Hilltop Point in the eastern mountain range that is contained by an earthen dam. It is a seasonal tourist resort area. Although Hilltop Point is not within the city limits, its commercial importance to the Ridgevale's economy cannot be overstated. Vacationers come down to the city during the day to shop, and in the evenings for dinner and entertainment. The Stacey County airport is in the valley on the outskirts of Ridgevale. It is a non-commercial, civil aviation facility.

In the city, there is the 120 acre Citizens Park, which is a densely wooded area transversed by pedestrian walkways and bicycle paths. It serves as a virtual buffer between the residential and industrial zones. Situated alongside the northeast sector of the park is the Edison Company electrical substation that serves the City of Ridgevale. Aside the northwest periphery is the regional water treatment plant.

Ridgevale's emergency service divisions (police, fire, EMS, and OEM) are fully-paid organizations consisting of the staffing levels in Table 3.

During your interview with the city's OEM director, you learn that the duties of deputy director include assessing the city's special hazard threats, preparing emergency response procedures, and training emergency service personnel. The responsibilities are clear and concise. You are further advised that the city is in danger of being fined several hundred thousand dollars if the Disaster Management Plan operational protocols are not updated and brought into compliance with state and federal mandates by the end of the year. The

Table 3.   Ridgevale's Emergency Service Divisions

Unit	Sworn Members	Civilian Employees
Police	312	47
Fire	155	24
EMS	59	0
OEM	0	6

The Department of Public Works employs 96 men and women.

Disaster Management Plan you are required to submit to the state for approval must include a set of recommendations to surmount each special hazard threat you identify. It is August. If you accept the position as DD/OEM, you must begin at once. To you, the predicament is not insurmountable. You know you have the qualifications, experience, and the energy that will be necessary to get the job done. You enthusiastically accept the offer, and in two weeks will be Ridgevale's new Deputy Director of Emergency Management.

Given the aforementioned set of responsibilities, how will you begin the evaluation process? When considering "special hazards threats," what is likely to occur that could impact on the safety and security of the people who live, work, and visit the city? How will you identify the training needs of each of the city's emergency service departments as well as other municipal department(s) that will be mobilized when the Disaster Management Plan is implemented?

Nineteen

Creative Financing: A New Source for Funding Essential Services

The telephone in your office seemingly has not stopped ringing since the county executives announced proposed legislation that will require a person to pay a sum of money each time he or she utilizes the Candiss County Emergency Medical Services. The intent of the proposition is to bill health care insurers for the rendered services. Even though there is a subheading entitled, "Ability to Pay" that would forgive those who do not have medical coverage, the people are nevertheless enraged, particularly the senior citizens. To you, the purpose of the proposed county regulation makes perfect sense. Non-county residents traveling through or visiting the region frequently utilize EMS services free of charge. This circumstance passes the cost along to county taxpayers. Since costs associated with mobile intensive care resources are escalating (i.e., helicopter evacuations, specialized response units), a tax increase in the near future is a *fait accompli*.

By billing insurance companies, the county will be able to recover monies to be earmarked for an emergency apparatus replacement fund as provided by the proposed law. Remuneration will actually stabilize the county's fiscal condition and obviate the need for a tax increase. As a result, apparatus purchases will be removed from the county's capital improvement fund. In sum, the system will virtually pay for itself.

The proposed legislation has been reported by both local and regional newspapers. It was a special feature on the evening television news, and it received extensive coverage on local radio stations as well. There are no hidden agendas. It is all really quite clear. But why are the people so upset? As Director of Candiss County Emergency Medical Services, you must quickly determine the reason for the distress and patch things up before the forthcoming county executive board meeting when the proposed legislation is up for a vote. What went wrong in the first place? How will you fix it?

59

Twenty

The Express Elevator to the Top Floor: Hop Aboard!

It is 8:30 A.M., and you can't stop staring at the front page of the morning's newspaper; it is suitable for framing: "FORD APPOINTED ASSISTANT COMMISSIONER OF HEALTH." The headline has eye appeal because *you* are Tom Ford, the newly appointed assistant commissioner.

Upon graduating from the university with an advanced degree in public administration, you began a promising career with the Garrison County Health Department. Once considered a rising star in the organization, advancement has been painfully slow. In fact, you have advanced only one pay grade since entering the department nine years ago. Your only position of status has been that of union shop steward, a position held until your recent promotion. Advancement to the unclassified and exempt position of Assistant Commissioner means that you have bypassed nine titled pay grades, leapfrogging over 75 classified employees of the department. The uproar has been far worse than you ever could have imagined. Your coworkers are incensed, particularly since they know that your mother, Dr. Karen Ford, was recently appointed Garrison County Executive Secretary.

The rumor of nepotism has been circulating through the department. For those in the agency, it is far too much of a coincidence. Many of those who occupy higher positions, including the three directors who you presently outrank, feel betrayed by your elevation. Each believes he or she is more qualified for advancement; every one of them has more experience and seniority as well.

It has been less than 24 hours since the press release announcing your promotion became the topic of shocked conversation among health department employees. It feels like a ceiling has collapsed, and you are trapped underneath the debris. What should be a time of joy and celebration is turning into a real-life horror motion picture with you as the star of the show. Your swearing-in ceremony is to take place at 3:00 P.M. in the commissioner's office. Your wife and two children will be in attendance. You begin to worry that they may be in for a hostile reception. Worse, your mother and father will also attend. In fact, your dad, Judge Robert Ford will swear you in as Assistant Commissioner. In your heart, you know this is not going to go over well with your colleagues.

By lunch time, your new secretary confides that she has requested a transfer to another office. She also tells you that the rank and file employees have planned some sort of a demonstration or job action in opposition to your promotion. She does not have additional information on the protest. Lastly, she indicates that the executive staff (three directors and eight division supervisors) plans to submit a letter to the county executives and the governor detailing their objections to your promotion. You expect the letter will be published in the newspaper as well, which will result in further embarrassment to you and your family. What is more, these are the people who will be reporting directly to you. How on this earth is this organizational relationship going to work in view of the unfolding circumstances?

By 1:00 P.M., you are formally notified in writing that the union representing county employees has petitioned an administrative law judge to temporarily set aside your promotion. The union is demanding immediate justification for the advancement in view of the circumvention of so many qualified employees. Once more, it seems like the sky is falling. What else can go wrong in such a short period of time?

By 2:15 P.M., you receive the answer to your question. County Health Commissioner Marvin Brooks intends to announce his retirement this afternoon to be effective at the end of the current fiscal year. Since you will be serving at the pleasure of the commissioner in your new post, you are faced with two obvious possibilities: 1) A newly appointed commissioner may not want you on his or her staff, and consequently; 2) You may eventually be returned to your titled civil service position. You balance these consequences against the probability that the county executives will not permit a new commissioner to demote you given your political connections. But wait . . . perhaps *you* may be named commissioner!

The title of Assistant Commissioner and the corresponding salary increase of $22,000 is not something to set aside because some people are hurt and upset. You also acknowledge that it will be difficult to command the respect of your coworkers, regardless of their positions in the organization. Getting things done in the short term will be a difficult. Over the long haul, bad feelings hopefully will dissipate, and everyone will get back to the business of public service.

Although deep in thought, you still can't take your eyes off of the headlines. Are you willing to ride out the storm, or do you decline the promotion and return to the comfort zone of your previous title? Will you be able to tough it out for the time necessary to heel the wounds of your fellow workers? What are some of the things you can do right away to ameliorate the situation for yourself and the organization?

Twenty-One

Stepping Up to the Plate: Decision Time in Birchwood Park

Birchwood Park is an old industrial city with a population of 23,646. It encompasses an area of 12 square miles. Once the mills closed, the city was in a state of depression for almost 10 years until University Hospital announced plans to construct a medical center and nursing school on four square blocks in the downtown business district. Soon other commercial establishments opened, and the city was once again vibrant. As recently appointed City Managing Director, you are pleased to enter the municipal government at this point in its history. Bad economic times are in the past. Things are certainly looking much better in terms of the city's tax base. Like most venues on the planet earth, however, the city is not without its issues and controversies.

The city has just celebrated the 75th anniversary of its beloved Memorial Stadium, the home of the Birchwood Park Stingers Independent Baseball League team. The facility is situated on a tract of city-owned property that is designated for "future" commercial development. The estimated value of the land is $3,000,000. Although the 4,000 seat stadium is the city's signature landmark, it is antiquated, in disrepair, and does not satisfy the mandated requirements for compliance with the Americans with Disabilities Act. Any reconstruction initiative must also include the installation of a state of the art fire suppression system, all of which will represent a sizeable expense to the taxpayers. Insurance costs have also escalated considerably in the last three years, and there is every indication that this outlay will continue to spiral. What is more, attendance has been in decline for several years.

Stadium workers are unionized city employees, and their salaries and medical benefits are increasing faster that the city's ability to pay. All of these consequences will necessitate a significant tax increase if the stadium is to continue to operate. Worse yet, the stadium has a reputation as being a nest for political sinecures. The latter perception alone will more than likely make a stadium-related proposed tax increase unacceptable.

Because there is no advertising in the stadium, the city is deprived of monies that could defray operating expenses. After all, who would want to pay for commercial advertising in a half-empty ball park? Other than Stinger baseball games and an annual, one-day high school marching band competition, there are very few other events in the stadium throughout the year.

The city would like to get out of the stadium business, sell the property, and use the money for capital improvement projects that include financing for an addition to the library, construction of a senior citizen recreation center, and land acquisition for four additional neighborhood playgrounds that could be purchased through a state grant with municipal matching funds. For at least five years, the public has been demanding that these projects get underway. On Election Day last year, the city included a non-binding referendum on the ballot giving its nearly 18,000 registered voters the opportunity to signify whether or not they would support a bond issue to keep the stadium open for business during the ensuing decade. The vote was a virtual 50-50 tie: 8,854 for and 8,831 against.

This year the city included a questionnaire in its residential tax billing mail out asking the citizens of Birchwood Park for their input on the stadium issue. Once again, half of the residents indicated that they would support a bond issue to upgrade the stadium and keep the ball park open. For at least half of the city's population, the stadium is a symbol of civic pride and tradition; it posses a sentimental value that cannot be expressed in dollars. Many residents wrote stories of their families (grandparents, parents, and later their own children) going to watch the Stingers play baseball; a tradition they are not in favor of ending.

One feature of the stadium is even considered sacrosanct. The interior wall along the first base side of the lower level corridor includes the historic Wall of Honor, which is a memorial to all of the city's veterans who fought and died for their country on battlefields that date from the Civil War. A structural engineer recently inspected the building and reported that the edifice was sound. However, the engineer's report concluded that if the building is to be demolished, the Wall of Honor could not be retained. Opposition voters see no reason the city should be managing a sports facility when the money could be better spent on more important undertakings. Even those who oppose extending the life of the stadium insist the Wall of Honor somehow be preserved, however.

As Managing Director, it is your job to make a recommendation to the city council on stadium's future. All things considered, you must identify the middle ground and arrive at a conclusion that resolves the issue favorably for both factions. The city council awaits your proposal.

Twenty-Two

The Coach Evan P. Stocker Memorial: Boom or Bust for Peyton Township?

Three weeks ago a single engine, four-passenger, fixed-wing aircraft crashed onto a field in rural Peyton Township, a sprawling 54 square mile unincorporated municipality with a population of 740. The sole victim of the tragedy was the owner-pilot of the plane, the state college's head football coach, Evan P. Stocker. Coach Stocker was a proverbial household name in the state. Although known primarily for his extraordinary career winning percentage at the state college, Coach Stocker had been involved in fund raising activities for several charities, and was also recognized for his volunteer work with underprivileged children. He recently received the coveted Morris Hoffman Medal of Excellence, an award that is considered the state's highest honor. Coach Stocker is survived by his wife of 44 years, three sons, two daughters, and eleven grandchildren. In sum, Stocker was an icon in the state.

Investigators determined the cause of the crash to be the result of engine failure. This circumstance made Coach Stocker's heartbreaking death that much more difficult to accept; it was not due to pilot error or to the imprudent decision to fly in extreme weather conditions. Both latter situations are naturally blamed exclusively on the pilot. Typically, mechanical failure is considered to be the fault of "something else."

Within hours of the public announcement of Coach Stocker's tragic death, mourners throughout the region began pilgrimages to the crash site bearing flowers, football team tee shirts, hats, helmets, and other like-items to be placed at the accident spot out of respect for their fallen hero. Before the end of the first week, thousands of people had visited the location. The field became a *de facto* memorial to Coach Stocker.

Lately, the governor is considering a proclamation that would dedicate the crash site as a permanent memorial to Coach Stocker. An overwhelming majority of state residents welcome the governor's declaration. However, the vast majority of Peyton Township residents do not agree with the governor on this issue.

Peyton Township is a tranquil place to live. Its rolling hills, winding narrow roads, expansive green acres, and two bird sanctuaries add to the quality of life for residents who long ago escaped city life for the quiet wilderness of Peyton Township. They too admired Evan Stocker and want to honor the memory of the state's greatest football coach. They are deeply saddened over his death, even more so because the crash occurred in their rural community. Their objection to a permanent memorial does not imply ambivalence or disrespect. They simply want to maintain the living standards that made Peyton Township so attractive.

Proponents of the initiative insist that some controlled commercial development will be good for Peyton. A memorial site will encourage manageable growth within a confined district that will benefit the residents. No longer will they need to travel a considerable distance to purchase household commodities. Property tax reductions may result as well. Township's residents nevertheless argue that a permanent memorial will bring hundreds of visitors to the area each month. They fear the whole concept of a permanent memorial is a virtual slippery slope issue, and are convinced that noise, pollution, traffic, and litter will be likely by-products of the project. They are concerned that the field will be transformed into a commercial zone dotted with sports-related souvenir shops and fast food restaurants. To the residents, the commercialization of someone's death is appalling.

Resident concerns are certainly understandable. But what about the huge margin of state residents who support the concept of a permanent memorial? Why should a township of less than 800 residents have veto power over the wishes of a majority of citizens? Furthermore, the typical slippery slope argument ("The sky is falling!") rarely has merit, and most non-residents believe it should be dismissed as a fatally flawed line of reasoning. In reality, interest in the crash site is likely to lessen over a relatively short period of time. One wonders why township residents would want to subject themselves to this emotionally-charged controversy and its highly exaggerated outcomes anyway. It all seems quite unnecessary.

In any event, the decision will be made in faraway Ebbettsville, the Oxford County seat of government having jurisdiction over Peyton Township. The county commissioners are of the same political party as the governor, and they have received some pressure from the capitol city to approve a permanent memorial site. They realize the political consequences that will likely result if they decide to deny the zoning variance required for the Stocker memorial. At the same time, the commissioners know equally well that there are enough votes among Peyton Township residents to systematically turn each of them out of office in future election cycles if they approve the variances.

As Oxford County's Chief Zoning Officer, what will be your recommendation to the commissioners that will most likely resolve the controversy?

Twenty-Three

The SLFD's Bravest: We're Not Yellow!

San Louisa is a 15 square mile city located in the southwestern United States with a population of 128,654. The downtown area consists of 14 square blocks of commercial establishments, the tallest structure being eight stories. Large industrial and manufacturing facilities are located in the city's outer ring area. San Louisa is also the headquarters of the Adobe County's school administration. The school system consists of nine schools (kindergarten through high school), all located within the city limits. Children are transported throughout the city during the school year aboard a fleet of 22 conventional school busses. The city is known for its year-round dry and sunny climate with an average temperature of 74 degrees. It has numerous Native American villages just outside of the center city area that attract thousands of tourists annually.

Early last year, Battalion Chief David Proctor of the city's fire department was promoted to the rank of Second Assistant Chief and immediately chaired the organization's apparatus committee. The *ad hoc* group consists of two firefighters, three line officers, one administrative officer, and one union representative. Their job is to meet periodically and review manufacturer's specifications for mobile fire fighting equipment. When the city's yearly capital budget is being prepared, the chair is expected to present the committee's recommendation for fleet acquisitions for the next fiscal year.

Chief Proctor assumed his new title and responsibilities at the outset of the budget preparation process. There was no time for the apparatus committee to abandon its anticipated forthcoming proposal and start over. Instead, the apparatus purchasing plan was presented to the city's Chief Financial Officer in its current format, with one exception. Chief Proctor insisted that the paint specifications be changed from the traditional red to an innovative yellow color. He suggested that the soon-to-be-acquired fire engines (4) be assigned one each to the city's four fire department battalions.

Chief Proctor wanted to evaluate the "Safety Yellow" concept for two years, the interim period before the next set of recommendations were to be advanced during budget meetings. All of the members serving on the apparatus committee disagreed with the proposed change in color. The crux of the dissenting argument centered on tradition; fire engines must always be painted red. Besides, one committee member observed, having yellow fire engines in San Louisa was like having white police cars at the North Pole! The Fire Chief accepted Proctor's reasoning and authorized the next delivery of apparatus to be painted yellow with the understanding that it was to be a test of appliance visibility. The intent of the change was understandable as well as admirable. Innovation and firefighter safety should prevail over any argument in favor of maintaining outdated traditions. Nevertheless, not a single member of the fire department was in favor of the change.

Once the four fire engines were placed in-service, the evaluation began. On its fifth emergency response, Engine Company 9, nicknamed the "Yellow Jacket," was involved in a two-vehicle collision with a passenger car. Although the passenger vehicle sustained significant property damage, no one was seriously injured, and the fire engine incurred minor body damage. Two days later, Engine Company 5, another yellow appliance, was struck by a large commercial truck while operating at a fire hydrant. Both vehicles sustained major damage; two firefighters suffered relatively minor injuries, although they were out of work for several weeks. Three months passed before another yellow fire engine was involved in a collision. On this occasion, the apparatus "t-boned" a passenger car at a major downtown intersection. Several civilians and firefighters were injured.

During the succeeding eight months, five more traffic accidents occurred involving the yellow apparatus. Fortunately, they were relatively minor in nature. Throughout the length of the color experiment, only one accident occurred involving a fire engine that was painted the traditional red color. At 3:00 A.M., on one rainy morning, an intoxicated driver struck the rear of Hook & Ladder Company 2 while it was stopped at a traffic signal. The Director of Training for the San Louisa Fire Department could not assign blame to any driver involved in a collision while operating one of the yellow fire engines. Each chauffeur had received both the basic and advanced emergency vehicle operator's training, and each was a veteran member of the department with no less than six years of experience on the job. Moreover, every department vehicle is equipped with state of the art audible and visual warning devices. What is more, drivers of red painted apparatus had not been involved in a single crash that could be attributed to operator carelessness during the same period.

The experiment was costly. The city was being sued for personal injury and property damage by the victims of what department members were calling "Yellow Fever." Already, nearly $800,000 is settlement costs were being paid to injured civilians. Workers Compensation and medical costs for the injured firefighters was also substantial.

Even Chief Proctor, a proponent of the safety yellow color, was bemused. By the end of the fiscal year, he was convinced that changing the apparatus color from red to yellow had been a mistake. But what went wrong? How could a color that is highly visible in all-weather, twenty-four hours a day, 365 days a year, effectively contribute to an increase in fire engine accidents?

Because fire department members have a bias for red colored fire engines (part of the service's custom and tradition), it was decided that a neutral party should be loaned to the organization to determine the possible causes(s) of the accidents in which yellow apparatus had been involved. You are temporarily transferred from your civil service position in the San Louisa Police Department's Traffic Safety Unit to carry out this review for the fire department. Where will you begin the investigation? Who will you interview? What will be the likely conclusion of your inquiry, and can you provide corresponding recommendation(s)?

Twenty-Four

A Tale of Two Cities: It Is the Best of Times, and the Worst of Times

With apologies to Charles Dickens, we begin the scenario with a brief history of the twin cities of North Adamson and South Adamson. A property dispute arose over territory settled by the Adamson family in the mid-1800s. Since there are no known written family memoranda or public records that reveal Donald, Sr. and Jessica Adamson's wishes for the property upon their deaths, the groundwork was in place for the approaching disagreement between their two surviving sons. Donald, Jr. and David Adamson, descendants of the original property owners, disagreed on potential future development opportunities for their 17 square mile land mass. Donald Adamson's vision was to join in the entrepreneurial spirit of capitalism sweeping the country and sell the land to developers who would transform the terrain from farmland to an urban center. David Adamson wanted no part of the risk associated with venture capitalism. Instead, he sought to maintain the territory as an agricultural—residential settlement; a concept he thought would be a low risk, high reward enterprise.

The nearest village, at the time of the argument, was the Town of Chesterfield, 15 miles south of the Adamson cattle ranch. David envisioned Chesterfield to be the urban center of the region. He was certain Chesterfield would grow substantially in the near future because of its location, which was along the proposed route of the Intercontinental Railroad. As Chesterfield grew, people would need a safe place to live in harmony and tranquility away from the workplace. Competing with Chesterfield would be irresponsible and foolish. Donald believed otherwise. Now is the time, he thought, to make a move that would relegate Chesterfield to just another jerk water stop along the railroad, if there was even going to be a railroad after all.

The hostility between the brothers gained momentum over time as neither refused to back down from their respective positions nor seek a reasonable

70

compromise that might settle the dispute. The only alternative was to equally divide the land between the two brothers, each having legal ownership of 8.5 square miles. The present-day difficulties that threaten the financial and social stability of the twin cities are a direct result of the Adamson brother's conflict that occurred during the post-Civil War period.

Donald's 8.5 square miles was named North Adamson; David's became South Adamson as a result of their geographic position in the region. North Adamson is today the urban center that was Donald's dream. The city has a population of 42,583 of which 56% is non-white. The downtown area is home to numerous commercial establishments: retail businesses, office towers, restaurants, and entertainment and sport facilities that stabilize its tax base. Its transportation system is rated as among the finest in the region. Residents consider public safety services to be excellent. Civic pride is manifested in the bragging rights that are usually granted to cosmopolitan cities. A significant shortcoming is the diminishing quality of education in the North Adamson School District. The district can no longer afford after-school programs or traditional extracurricular activities. Five teacher positions have been eliminated in the past year as well. The union representing the teachers has threatened to strike if the positions are not restored before the next school year. There is even conjecture among city officials that the recent increase in juvenile crime and disorderly conduct is the result of deteriorating conditions in the schools. They wonder if these cost-saving measures might warrant the hiring of additional police officers, which would be far more expensive. The worse case scenario would be for crime to increase, which could drive businesses out of the city. Bad schools and criminal misconduct join to create a formula for calamity.

Increasing costs have also forced cutbacks in the city's Department of Public Works. Trash and recycling pick-ups have been reduced from bi-weekly to weekly. Streets are rarely swept, and many are in disrepair as the city struggles to maintain its current tax rate. North Adamson wants no part of raising taxes that typically cause residents and businesses to flee North American cities.

Meanwhile, South Adamson is everything that David foresaw decades earlier. It is a city of picturesque residential subdivisions with excellent neighborhood schools, community swimming pools and recreation centers, quaint strip malls, tall trees, and a few remaining farms. Its streets are well maintained, and shade trees along both sides of most of the city streets provide a green tunnel-like cover. It is an attractive residential community for the reasons specified. It takes satisfaction in knowing that North Adamson has a few dozen "defectors" every year who resettle in South Adamson. Bragging rights for the insular city, no doubt. As with most cities that are primarily residential, South Adamson does not have the attractions of an urban center like North Adamson. Nor does the city have a public funded transportation system. Privately owned vehicles are the primary mode of transportation. Its tax base is 94% homeowner, 6% commercial. The population of the city increases about two percent annually with a current population of 31,456; 18% are non-white. One of the remaining farms is for sale, and it is expected a housing developer will purchase the property. As previously indicated, there are virtually no commercial ratables in South Adamson. Although public safety services are considered to be below federal, state, and regional standards (perhaps dangerously so), there is absolutely no desire on the part of South Adamson residents to upgrade the present level of services. There is no support for another annual tax increase.

In sum, North Adamson does not want to be akin to South Adamson. Likewise, South Adamson doesn't want to be anything like North Adamson. The dispute continues. Chesterfield, meanwhile, remains the small town it was in the 1800s. The Transcontinental Railroad right-of-way is 97 miles north of the municipality.

Recently, a private citizen, Edwin Donhart, took to the microphone during a North Adamson city council meeting and proposed to resolve each city's predicaments by means of shared services contracts. In so doing, each city would maintain its strengths and, concomitantly, eliminate its weaknesses. Mr. Donhart was literally booed and shouted down, forcing him to retreat from the microphone. He never had the opportunity to present his case in an organized manner. As a matter of fact, he wasn't even afforded the courtesy to offer an outline or framework for his idea. It seems that old disputes never die. North Adamson City Council Member Frank Morton thought the idea had merit and wanted to pursue it further.

Political consequences not withstanding, Morton contacted citizen Donhart to learn more about his suggestion. After doing so, Morton contacted South Adamson City Council Member Janet Higginson. Morton proposed to work informally and confidentially with her to formulate a scheme that might be palatable to both constituencies. Because Morton and Higginson were members of the same political party and had been classmates at St. George College, neither would feel uncomfortable about engaging in off-the-record discussions. Furthermore, both understood the gravity of the situation. To do nothing would acerbate the already undesirable conditions each city is presently experiencing. Morton and Higginson decide to formulate a plan to regionalize selected services between their respective cities. Later, they will jointly present their proposal to the individual city councils.

What services need to be regionalized? Which services may be able to be regionalized with a minimum of effort? What consequences will likely result if conditions remain *status quo* in each city? What will the Morton-Higginson strategy recommend? How will they forestall the foreseeable political repercussions?

Will the ghosts of the Adamson brothers triumph once again? Or will a far, far better thing be done than has ever been done before?

Twenty-Five

The Clash between Idealism and Realism: Or, "They Never Taught Me about the P-word in College"

The Business Administrator in Town of Dunston (population 6,022) recently graduated with honors from Blue Hill College where he received a Bachelor of Arts degree in Public Administration. Interviews for the position had been conducted by the Town Council and outgoing Business Administrator. When completed, Ken Robb emerged as the most qualified applicant to fill the vacancy. He impressed everyone with his insight and ability to articulate his vision for the town's future. Best of all, he had no political anchor around his neck.

Small town USA is the typical launch pad for people like Ken Robb who intend to pursue a career in the public sector. Like so many others, he aspires to gain experience, continue his education, network with other town administrators, and use the knowledge accrued as leverage to move on to larger municipalities with greater challenges. For now, he wants to do his very best for Dunston. Once hired, he would have complete management control of and the authority and responsibility for the day-to-day functions of the municipal government.

Ken Robb began by interviewing the town's seven full-time employees. He wanted to listen to their ideas so he could formulate a plan to eliminate any perceived weakness(es) in the administration and operation of their respective departments. One flaw in the system quickly became evident: each staff member objected to the custom of relying on a part-time employee for the procurement of their office supplies. Although the current practice is the result of a money saving initiative that began eight years earlier, each thought the practice was inefficient and wasteful. Moreover, some office supply needs are time-sensitive. Waiting a month for needed goods can have a deleterious effect on employee productivity as well as service delivery to the public.

Once each month, the part-time employee, Mary Harmonson, collects purchasing requests from each office in town hall. During a typical 30-day period, each department head tracks the office supply inventory and submits a request form for needed merchandise. Thereafter, purchase orders are prepared by the part-timer and forwarded to the Business Administrator for review, and then to the Town Council for the ultimate approval or rejection. All seven staff members want to have responsibility for their own purchases. Ken thought this was a reasonable request. His first decision was to approve the decentralization of purchasing. His staff was delighted. He was off to a good start as far as they were concerned. He dismissed the part-time employee, a retired senior citizen, who earned an annual salary of $513.60 for her eight hours per month or 96 hours annually at $5.35 hourly rate of pay.

In the world of public service, reality has a sobering effect on people. Ken was summoned by Mayor Cheryl Hall, herself a senior citizen and part-time member of the town council, to account for his unilateral decision to decentralize purchasing. When questioned, his first defense was that he had been directed to take whatever action deemed necessary and appropriate for the efficient and effective administration and management of the government. Ken actually believed he was the ultimate authority in the Town of Dunston. Ken had not considered the "p-word" when he made the decision.

First, as the mayor pointed out, a trustworthy and valuable staff member, albeit a part-time employee, had been dismissed without cause. Legal as well as political consequences were likely to result. Second, before the reduction in force went into effect eight years earlier, Mary Harmonson had been the town's purchasing agent. When she retired, the position was eliminated. Third, why wasn't Mary Harmonson interviewed before the decision was made to dismiss her? After all, each full-time employee had been questioned. Finally, personnel decisions *before* they are made should be brought to the attention of each town council member for their consideration and comment.

Mayor Hall saw this situation as an opportunity for Ken Robb to learn the ways and means of properly running a town, the "reality" he did not receive in the college classroom. She offered the following observations:

- Administrative, technical, *and* political (the "p-word') issues must be carefully analyzed before a final decision is made;
- In the present case, the lack of a centralized purchasing protocol adds to the cost of commodities as well as the administrative costs associated with the process;
- A decentralized procurement system is a fragmented process that limits budget control management while at the same time driving up overall costs; and

• Regardless of the legal mandates of your office, *always* keep elected officials in the loop.

Although psychologically wounded, Ken appreciated the mayor's insightful remarks. He had tried to do the right thing. Upon somber reflection, he fully understands that a lack of experience and political acumen resulted in a serious error in judgment.

What steps must he take to repair the damage? Is he likely to lose the respect of the seven staff members if he reverses the decision? Is reversing the decision the only viable alternative? How will you mend Mary Harmonson's wounded sensibilities?

Twenty-Six

Building the "Big Box"
or "Green Side Up"?:
Thomasville's Zoning Predicament

Fifteen square mile Thomasville Township (population 28,963) is situated on the edge of Thornton, a seven square mile city with a population of 81,222. Presently, township planners and council members are considering a proposal from the Mega Thrift Mart Company to construct a mammoth super store at the Pettus Junction Shopping Center that would replace a vacant strip store shopping plaza currently on the site.

City representatives from nearby Thornton are lobbying state, county, and local Thomasville officials on behalf of the construction project that will create an anticipated 100-plus jobs, most of which will likely be filled by their city residents. In addition to job creation, Thornton residents will benefit from access to the discount giant's affordable merchandise not presently available anywhere in the city. Thomasville will benefit from the desperately needed commercial tax ratable that will help pay for the ever-increasing cost of municipal services. The proposed development will likely be an economic benefit to the entire region.

Opponents of the project argue that construction of a Mega Thrift Mart will harm small businesses in the township as well as those in neighboring Thornton. They imply that businesses within a four mile radius will be in jeopardy of failing. Job and ratable losses may actually be greater than the proposed plan is intended to create. Yet, they offer no real evidence (data or testimony) in support of their assumptions.

Residents of the Fox Hunt neighborhood adjacent to the project site are concerned about construction noise, dust and dirt, and the likelihood of an overall decline in their quality of life. They site post-construction "people noise," traffic congestion, and litter as additional long term annoyances. Indeed, Fox Hunt homeowners are the most vocal critics of the proposal. Fox

Hunt residents also object to the state and county highway reconstruction that will be required to facilitate safe and easy access to the shopping center. They contend that additional taxes will be needed to fund roadway improvements and submit that the Mega Thrift Mart Company should pay for the required upgrading. Mega Thrift Mart representatives have indicated they will abandon their construction plans should the company be made to fund highway improvements.

Marvin Kipp, Esq., president of the Fox Hunt Civic Association has issued a virtual call to arms to neighborhood residents. Kipp believes the construction project has been forced on the community because the overwhelming majority of subdivision registered voters cast their ballots in the recent municipal elections for the opposing political party, which failed to receive enough vote's township-wide to win the election. To Kipp, it is blatant political retribution.

Kipp contends that approval of the construction project violates the township's master plan. According to Kipp, once a municipality approves and submits its master building plan to the state there can be no changes for ten years, unless a variance application is approved by the state. No such variance approval has been received by any municipality in the past 16 years. Kipp has threatened to file a "stop work" injunction in the Superior Court should the project be approved. He plans to appeal the decision to the state's Department of Community Affairs. Case law, he contends, is on the side of the Fox Hunt residents.

Further research has revealed that Thomasville is mandated by the state's Green Acres Restoration Act to set aside 30 acres that are to be restored and maintained as public park lands. The proposed Mega Thrift Mart project is on a 31.5 acre parcel of land, almost enough to satisfy the township's obligation. Kipp will file an additional suit to force the township to comply with the state mandate should construction be approved.

Two politically powerful organizations have joined Marvin Kipp and his neighbors in opposing the Mega Thrift Mart project: the America Legion and the Veterans of Foreign Wars. Pettus Junction Shopping Center is named after the city's World War II resident silver and bronze star medal recipient, Major John Herbert Pettus, Jr. Both veteran organizations are advocating for the construction of a statue of Pettus that will be the centerpiece of a new park and recreation complex. Each organization has pledged to raise the necessary funds for the sculpture and surrounding landscape at no cost to the township. Naturally, Kipp et al. are encouraged by the unexpected alliance.

A scientific public opinion poll conducted on behalf of the Thomasville public officials reveals that a majority of township residents favor construction of the Mega Thrift Mart for numerous reasons, a main concern being the generation of tax revenue from the commercial enterprise that will benefit the public at large. Mayor Evan Gordon, Council President Sheilla Mester, and three of the five members of the township council are in favor of the project. They also realize they are in for a fight; politically, in the courts, and before the Department of Community Affairs in the state capital. Protests are anticipated that will likely require the police department to provide 24-hour coverage at the site at considerable cost to the taxpayers. Legal fees to defend the township against expected law suits will likewise come at a great expense.

If the township is required to refurbish the site as a municipal park, it will become its fulltime caretaker. The grounds must be maintained. Security must be provided 24/7. Pathways must be created to facilitate bicycle riding and walking. A water system must be installed to service fountains and facilitate lawn watering during the summer season. Trash receptacles must be purchased, placed in the park, and waste removal provided. Electricity for lighting is essential, and expensive. Insurance costs will rise. Small wonder why most township residents support the Mega Thrift Mart project.

But what about the vocal "minority?" As Thomasville's chief planner the mayor and council have instructed you to sort out the strengths, weaknesses, opportunities and threats, and the costs and benefits of both options. You will present your findings and conclusions at a special hearing on the proposed project. It will be an open meeting. You can expect advocates for both sides in the dispute to be present in force. What should Thomasville do as far as the Mega Thrift Mart proposal is concerned? Is there a middle ground somewhere in these competing agendas? Is there another alternative that could meet the needs of the community?

Twenty-Seven

Something for the Both of Us?
Or A Problem for One of Us?

Greenfield Borough is renowned for its wealthy residents, luxurious homes, beautifully landscaped properties, clean streets, and a responsive municipal government. Although only three square miles in size with a population of 6,174, it is considered the political powerbase of the region. The current governor is a Greenfield resident. A state representative and a member of the United States Congress also own homes in this prestigious community. Medical doctors, attorneys, investment bankers, and other professionals make their homes in Greenfield.

The borough has no commercial ratables, and it doesn't need any. A combination elementary, middle, and high school campus complex is the community's principle showpiece nestled among the evergreens on Green Tree Street, the borough's main thoroughfare. It is a quiet, peaceful, and safe place to live. Property taxes are understandably very high, with the typical homeowner paying about $13,000 annually in property taxes.

Greenfield is literally encircled by the eleven square mile City of Ramsgate, population 24,022. Like Greenfield, Ramsgate is considered an upscale community. It has three enclosed shopping malls and a town center with shops on each side of its main street. Both attract hundreds of residents daily from the surrounding towns and villages.

Although Greenfield and Ramsgate are each served separately by rival political parties, there has been some recent conversation, albeit informal, among public officials from both jurisdictions regarding the sharing of municipal services. Mayor Louis Hansberry of Greenfield and Mayor William Church of Ramsgate both think the idea has some merit and mutually agree to continue the discussion.

One of the problems foreseen by both mayors is the collective bargaining agreement between the unionized municipal employees of Ramsgate and the city. In and of itself, it is not a problem for Ramsgate public officials. It is, however, a problem for borough officials in Greenfield where municipal employees are non-union workers. Once the shared service discussions become public knowledge, Greenfield officials fear that the union will make an immediate further attempt to organize their municipal workforce, regardless of what agreement, if any, is reached on sharing services between the two communities.

Both municipalities believe they will benefit from a shared service agreement. Ramsgate will be the lead municipality and provide Greenfield with police, fire, emergency medical services, public works, and utility services. Ramsgate will receive the required and sufficient compensation from the borough for providing these necessary and vital services. If the agreement proceeds along the lines presently under discussion, Greenfield will eliminate all of its operating agencies. It will merge its six-member police force with the 36-member Ramsgate Police Department. Its volunteer fire and ambulance services will be eliminated. The two-station Ramsgate Fire and EMS Department will provide full coverage to the borough. Public works (nine employees) will also join together with the 21 employees of the Ramsgate Public Works and Utilities Department. All employees will be members of one unionized labor force.

Even with the proposed mergers, property taxes in Greenfield will not likely be reduced. A percentage of each homeowner's property tax assessment will be paid to Ramsgate as part of the shared services contract. It is anticipated that many Greenfield residents are likely to wonder why a shared services agreement is really necessary. After all, will they actually benefit from such an arrangement? If so, how? Will Ramsgate residents and business owners have a similar view?

There will be open public hearings on the proposal once conversations advance from the informal to formal phase. Mayors Hansberry and Church immediately agree on one thing; once formal dialogue and debate commence, technical and administrative issues and their corresponding political consequences will undoubtedly surface for both jurisdictions to seriously consider. They are of the same opinion that an independent consultant should be hired to determine what the fallout will likely be in advance of formal proceedings.

You have been selected to serve as consultant to the governing bodies of Greenfield and Ramsgate. As a retired regional planning director, your experience, academic credentials, and history of achievement are unparalleled in the state. You are tasked with the responsibility of making recommendations as to the feasibility of a shared services agreement, along with its concomitant opportunities and threats. Remember that you must carefully consider the technical, administrative, and political advantages and disadvantages for each municipality. What will be in your report?

By the way, there has been some indication that you will be hired to negotiate the shared service contract between the borough and the city if your preliminary report indicates that such an arrangement is feasible. If this "rumor" turns out to be true, you had better prepare a set of recommendations based on your findings in order to bring the matter to a successful and timely conclusion.

Twenty-Eight

Lost in Space: We Can't Find Julie Again

Each day of the five-day work week, the classified employees of the Inspectional Services Bureau of the Department of Occupational Safety and Health are assigned to perform unannounced safety audits of randomly selected public and private sector workplaces throughout the state. Inspection teams are comprised of three certified safety and health officials, one of which is designated as the team leader. Once the team departs from its central office in the state capital for its daily inspection regimen, it is all but separated from the agency for the entire workday.

On occasion, this routine is interrupted when one or more of the teams must immediately cease the routine inspections and respond to the scene of an emergency at another worksite. One problem has repeatedly surfaced when a team must be redirected to the scene of an emergency: all too often the team leader has difficulty mobilizing his or her team members in a timely fashion once they are dispersed and in the process of conducting routine inspections, particularly in large facilities.

In the course of a year, each of the nine teams is reassigned to the scene of an emergency an average of 30 times. During each of these contingencies, a minimum of 20 minutes are lost during the effort to assemble the team. These circumstances result in the cumulative loss of between 80 and 100 hours of annual productivity. This consequence is in part the result of the department's refusal to budget for cellular telephones that can be issued to each team member. The department objects to providing field workers with cellular telephones due to both the cost as well as the potential for employee misuse. As a result, inspection team members can be recalled or redirected by an electronic paging device (primitive by today's advanced technology) that is issued solely to each team leader.

Recently, team member Julie Powers could not be reached for 40 minutes when her team was redirected to the scene of a hazardous materials incident at a manufacturing plant nearly 20 miles from her pre-assigned location. Julie methodically and conscientiously continued her inspection protocol at Space Technologies, Inc., unaware of the emergent situation at hand. This incident and other similar ones caused several operational problems, the most significant of which is all too obvious: a delayed response to a critical incident obviates the advantage of working with other emergency responders at the early stages of the event. Observation and evidence collection at this interval is crucial to a successful and credible investigation as to the cause. An inordinate number of agency investigative reports are subject to question or outright refutation. As a result, imposed sanctions are too often overturned on appeal. A team's work effort, therefore, is repeatedly wasted.

You are a team member and a recent graduate of the state's Theorem Institute on Public Sector Productivity. You accept the institute's charge that its alumni return to their respective organizations and initiate procedures and processes that will improve productivity and service delivery to its constituents. Since Norman Wells, the Director of the Inspectional Services Bureau, is also a graduate and proponent of Theorem Institute programs, you decide to do something about the lost productivity issue in the department.

How will you apply the command, "do the math" to this case? How will you frame the argument, both qualitatively and quantitatively?

Twenty-Nine

Rosehill's Outreach Program: What We Have Here Is a Failure to Communicate

As Deputy School Superintendent in the small urban city of Rosehill, you are charged with the responsibility of recruiting faculty members that adequately reflect the municipality's diverse population. An examination of the latest census data pertaining to its demographics reveals that Rosehill's population is 60% white and 40% minority. The minority population consists of a relatively equal proportion of African-Americans, Hispanic-Americans, Asian-Americans, and Indian-Americans. The current teaching staff is predominantly white.

You realize the importance of having a faculty that looks like the people of Rosehill. You want the teachers to be role models for the children in the city's three grammar schools and its one high school. You are truly altruistic in your beliefs regarding the importance of having a multi-cultural staff. You also realize that a failure to attract qualified minority candidates might result in litigation and a court-mandated consent decree, particularly since 12 of the 37 predominantly white faculty members are eligible for retirement next year. You want to be ahead of the curve on both issues. Recruitment of minorities, therefore, is the obvious first step in any candidate selection process.

The actual selection process for teacher applicants has been consistent (and successful) for decades, and involves the following protocol: 1) Submission of a formal application and resume; 2) Background investigation in order to determine the applicant's *bona fides* and qualifications; 3) Written examination; and 4) Oral interview. Once more, recruitment must be focused on attracting qualified minority applicants.

First, you prepare a Notice of Employment Opportunity to the print and electronic media for immediate release. Next, you actively contact various civic associations, churches, political organizations, business associations, and like-groups within the minority communities in the city and region to encourage certified teachers to apply to the Rosehill School District for employment. You include information on starting salary (negotiable, based on experience), pay scales, and benefit packages (medical coverage and vacation leave). You personally reach out to minority teachers in surrounding school districts to encourage them to apply for employment in Rosehill.

The deadline arrives for applications to be received. After carefully reviewing each one to ascertain if qualifications are satisfied, you schedule the written examination portion of the selection process and notify each eligible applicant in writing of the time and location of the written examination. At the test site, you anxiously await the arrival of the candidates. Much to your disappointment and disbelief, only one minority applicant registers for the written exam. It seems as though the months of effort you put forth to recruit minority applicants failed in its objective.

Back in your office the following morning, you contemplate the failure. What went wrong? The telephone rings on your desk; it is the Chief Superintendent of Schools Eugene Giles on the line. He has just finished reading an editorial in the morning newspaper admonishing the district for its failure to attract and employ qualified minority teachers. The article suggests some negligence on the part of school district administrators and promises to further investigate the subject. Superintendent Giles directs you to prepare a report in defense of the district's effort to hire qualified minority candidates.

Again, you ask yourself the question, "What went wrong, if anything?"

Thirty

Along the Blue Light Highway: Migration or Revitalization?

Presidential Boulevard, commonly referred to by local residents as the "Blue Light Highway" because nine police departments patrol the thoroughfare, is a 16 mile-long, four-lane east-west corridor that transverses nine municipalities in suburban Hazlet County. Rapid expansion of the area began during the mid-1950s when developers purchased hundreds of acres of land adjacent to the highway for the purpose of constructing housing subdivisions in each of the nine towns.

The demand for single-family housing was a function of the progression of commercial development along the boulevard. Simply stated, people tend to follow the jobs. Numerous corporate parks, medical offices, light manufacturing facilities, motels, and shopping centers seemingly materialized overnight. Gasoline service stations, car washes, banks, restaurants, and fast food chain eateries dotted the landscape. Job opportunities were plentiful across many occupations.

The nine contiguous communities situated alongside Presidential Boulevard were growing at about the same pace as the demand for municipal services, particularly public works and police, was increasing. Together, these local entities represent an area of 26.34 square miles, with an estimated aggregate resident population of 61,218. Each town has its own public works department, and each has its own police department. Fortunately, fire and ambulance services in each town are provided by trained neighborhood volunteers.

Each town also maintains its own grammar and middle school district. School bus service is provided by each town to their residents for grammar, middle, and high school students. The area's three public high schools are a part of the Hazlet County Regional School District. Hazlet County also maintains a county library system that provides educational services to each of its 22 municipalities.

These arrangements worked reasonable well for almost 32 years. Presently, however, each of the nine towns alongside Presidential Boulevard is built-out, and there is no land space available for the construction of additional commercial ratables. Residential property taxes are high in each town with the average homeowner paying $6,675. Likewise, commercial property taxes in each town are high, both due in large measure to the escalating cost of municipal government services. A few small businesses had recently closed and/or relocated due to rising costs. There are indications that some of the larger commercial enterprises are considering moving to other venues as well, perhaps outside of the county altogether. As commercial establishments incrementally go out of business or move somewhere else, residential property taxes are correspondingly raised in each of the nine municipalities. This condition has caused hundreds of people to sell their homes and leave the area.

Like the cascading effect of water flowing down a mountain, the nine "Presidential" towns are feeling the financial impact of this phenomenon. While the numbers of commercial ratables are gradually decreasing, the costs of municipal services continue to increase at an even faster pace. In four of the communities, collective bargaining agreements between the town and its police officers are set to expire in four months. In two other towns, negotiations are under way for new agreements with employees of the Public Works Department. The cost of rolling stock (cars and trucks) for both the Police Department and Public Works Department in all towns will increase by 6% just in time for forthcoming vehicle purchases.

The state has also mandated additional municipal funding for special education programs from kindergarten to the sixth grade. Teacher contracts will expire in three years in all of the boulevard towns as well. Some school buildings are in disrepair and will require major renovation almost immediately. Capital budget planning includes funding for fire apparatus purchases in five of the towns.

One town has a public golf course, and all taxpayers are members by virtue of their residency. Construction of a new clubhouse will be required within two years. The clubhouse serves as an entertainment center for a variety of recreational activities throughout the year. Wedding receptions are frequently held in the clubhouse. The proposed building expansion project will include a 5,000 square foot senior citizen's wing. Maintenance costs for the recreation facility are rising, and many of the small motorized vehicles (i.e., lawn mowers) need to be replaced. The cost of utilities is getting higher each year. There was some talk a few years ago of closing the golf course. The public outcry was such that closing the golf course was tantamount to political suicide. The town mayor put it succinctly when he said, "It ain't happening. Period!"

Each town has a small public park. So-called green zones are mandated by the state as a condition for building permit approvals when developers apply for land use variances for the construction of residential subdivisions. Maintenance of the parks cost each town a relatively small amount of money, and public officials don't seem to object to their preservation, although liability insurance costs are mounting.

To make matters worse, each of the nine towns recently received an ominous report from the Insurance Services Organization (ISO), a non-governmental agency that assesses fire protection and emergency service delivery. The ISO report warns that home and commercial fire insurance costs will increase exponentially unless each town employs two, full-time paid professional firefighters to staff their respective firehouses between the hours of 10:00 A.M. and 6:00 P.M. This stipulation is due to the declining number of volunteer firefighters available in each town and response time deficiencies associated with this condition during the indicated hours.

Because the problems facing these communities are regional, the mayors in each of the nine towns, all of whom serve part-time, have agreed to hold a conference in an effort to safeguard one or more of the towns from insolvency. Because of the precious tradition of home rule in the state, there is virtually no possibility that two or more of the towns will agree to join together. Amalgamation, therefore, will not be the subject of discussion at the forthcoming summit. Everything else is on the agenda. The mayor's conference in and of itself is an acknowledgement that something must change. That is a given. The challenge for the nine mayors is to find some points of agreement on how to avoid municipal bankruptcy and retain commercial and residential taxpayers. In sum, it is essential to stop the bleeding before the patient expires.

The mayors enter the meeting with the resolve to do something. Each mayor must move quickly to stabilize the tax rate in their town. They too fully appreciate the political consequences of proposing service cutbacks in their respective municipalities. After long hours of deliberation, they leave the assembly agreeing on one thing: the need for an independent study by a nonpartisan consulting firm. It is perhaps the best political and practical option available to them. They propose to contract with the Research Institute that is affiliated with the state university.

Ironically, you have just completed your course of study for a Masters Degree in Public Administration at the state university and are preparing a concept paper for your research thesis proposal. It is at this juncture that you learn of the situation that threatens the viability of the nine Presidential

Boulevard towns. You begin to think about writing your essay on the financial crisis that confronts the public officials in these municipalities. You understand that identifying the scope of the problem alone will not be enough to satisfy your thesis requirements.

You do some background work on the subject and learn of the mayor's conference and its outcome. You are ecstatic when you find out that the university will be contracted to conduct an evaluation and prepare a set of recommendations for review and consideration by the mayors. You decide to apply for an exemplarily project grant from the university's Research Institute to conduct the study by yourself. Two weeks later, you receive the letter that you have been eagerly awaiting. The university has approved the project, and your thesis research proposal has likewise been accepted. First, you must prepare a preliminary presentation that you will deliver before a joint meeting of the boulevard mayors outlining in general what you intend to examine. Of course, their agreement at that interval will be critical.

In the long term, your specific analysis will determine not only the success of the strategic plan you will recommend to the nine municipalities, but the success of your thesis project as well. You contemplate the challenges that lie ahead and begin to list each of one of them in their order of importance. If this were really *you*, what recommendations (general and specific) will your strategic plan likely contain? How will you go about conducting the research?

Thirty-One

The French Connection:
A Neighborhood's Tipping Point?

A day in the life of the Kedzie Township Code Enforcement Office can best be described as a four-aspirin-a-day experience made worse by recent staff reductions. The cutbacks were due in part to overestimated tax revenue projections that were not realized in the past year.

During the previous fiscal period, the township employed five certified and experienced code enforcement officers. This year, the staff has been reduced to three. Last year, the office inspected or investigated 2391 properties, many of which were the result of citizen complaints about inadequate commercial building maintenance, insufficient or unsatisfactory residential property maintenance in accordance with community standards, and complaints of building permits not displayed (or not issued). In addition, 388 property-related complaints were received that required an initial inspection by code enforcement officers that were subsequently referred to the township fire marshal's office for further investigation and resolution, bringing the figure to 2779 complaints processed.

The above figure (2779) does not include property inspections initiated by the office as a result of the 144 construction permits issued last year. In the final analysis, the five-person office conducted a total of 2923 inspectional services. This number represents an average of 585 inspectional services performed by each of the five code enforcement officers annually. The office processes over 243 complaints each month.

Inspectional services have increased annually by an average of seven percent over the previous ten years. This year the office anticipates an increase of 20 additional inspectional services that will need to be processed with two less code enforcement officers. Thus, the average case load per-employee will rise from 585 annually to 981, a seemingly impossible mission.

French Street is a one-block lane that transverses two major roadways in the 22.7 square mile township and is near the main boulevard entrance to the Forest Hill subdivision and home to 37 residents occupying 11 single family dwellings. For 55 years, French Street afforded its homeowners a good quality of life. However, conditions have been changing over the past two years, and the natives are getting restless.

When Mr. and Mrs. Harvey Sanders retired and moved to southern California, they sold their home for a quarter of century to a property management group. The property management group is a corporation that invests in residential property that they upgrade and lease to renters.

The lessee who took up residence in the Sanders' house is married with four young children. Soon after occupying the house, the renter placed a sign on the front lawn advertising his newly established exterminating business. Initially, the French Street residents were ambivalent about the sign. Their ambivalence didn't last long, however. Soon, large containers marked "pesticides" were observed alongside of the house and in the rear yard. This condition unnerved the residents for three reasons: 1) Young children were playing near the drums everyday; 2) Residents were concerned about the storage of hazardous materials in their neighborhood; and 3) Residents feared a decrease in their property values since the residential neighborhood had been a prime residential site in the city.

Before long, employees of the bug spraying company began to muster on the street at around 5:30 A.M. with their pick-up trucks and chemical repositories in tow. The early morning reveille quickly became a daily nuisance. A similar situation became part of the day by day routine. At 4:00 P.M., the crew of creepy crawler killers returned to French Street to "sign out" for the day's work during which time their equipment partially blocked the street as well as one or two residential driveways. Elevated noise levels contributed to the rapid decline in the quality of life on the street and the experience has been unpleasant to say the least.

Residents of French Street were never particularly active in community affairs. As expected, the diminution of traditional neighborhood standards got their attention, and several telephone calls were placed to the township Code Enforcement Office. Each caller received the same message from the office secretary: "The site will be added to our list."

Meanwhile, a family of four (Gloria and Bill Grasso and children) who has lived on the block for less than three years is planning to relocate from their small ranch house to a "two-decker" in a neighboring subdivision. It seems the little woman is expecting child number three, and larger quarters will be needed. The same investment group has placed a bid on the for-sale Grasso house higher than market value and more than has been offered by other prospective buyers. Once the neighbors became aware of this consequence, a virtual hell broke loose. They plan to object (and protest, if necessary) the sale to the investment group Together, residents will argue that current depreciating conditions on the block are a direct result of a privately owned dwelling having been converted to a rental property, and the good folks on French Street do not want more of the same.

To acerbate the existing state of affairs, one of the neighbors (Dan McNally), a 40-year resident of French Street, is so upset and frustrated over the present situation that he has announced a plan to sell his house to a motorcycle club at less than market value to "get even" with the township for allowing this undesirable condition to exist. "Why should I pay $4700 in property taxes to an uncaring and unresponsive municipal government?" questions McNally. You can be sure his threat to sell is genuine. He wants out of the area. Needless to say, this too is upsetting the residents. McNally has always impeccably maintained his property, and his house has always been an asset to the block and surrounding neighborhood.

Will French Street be the tipping point for the future of Forest Hill? Will one resident after the other put their homes up for sale? Will Forest Hill properties devalue rapidly block-by-block?

French Street property owners continue to call the Code Enforcement Office. If no response in forthcoming, they plan to call the Mayor's Office. Inaction will result in some form of protest—either at a township council meeting or some form of direct action on the block.

As Chief of the Code Enforcement Office, this situation could be a blessing in disguise for you. It could bring attention to the overworked and understaffed workforce. It may also cause the office to suffer some indignity (or worse!) if you fail to take action.

What direction is the best alternative? What "best option" scenario will you select, and what do you plan to do in either case?

Bibliography

Evers, Frederick T. & Rush, James C. "The Bases of Competence: Skill Development During the Transition from University to Work." *Management Learning,* 27(3), 1996.

Evers, Frederick T., Rush, James C. & Berdrow, I. *The Bases of Competence: Skills for Lifelong Learning and Employability*. San Francisco, CA: Jossey-Bass Publishers, 1998.

Held, W. G. (ed.). *Decisionmaking in the Federal Government: The Wallace Sayre Model*. Washington, D.C.: The Brookings Institution, 1979.

Jacobs, Jane. *The Death and Life of Great American Cities*. New York: Random House, 1961.

About the Authors

Robert J. Daniello is a retired municipal police executive. After serving 31 years in the Cherry Hill, New Jersey Police Department, he spent two years with the New Jersey State Treasury Department as a consultant to local government. He is now self-employed as an independent consultant.

Paulette Laubsch is a retired Assistant Commissioner in the New Jersey State Department of Labor where she served with distinction for 31 years. She is currently an Associate Professor at the School of Administrative Science, Farleigh-Dickenson University, Teaneck, N.J.

Robert and Paulette are Certified Public Managers in the State of New Jersey and have doctorates in Public Administration from Nova-Southeastern University in Broward County, Florida.